George Hugg

Rich in blessing

A grand new collection for Sunday-schools, Christian endeavor, Epworth League,

revival, camp and prayer meetings

George Hugg

Rich in blessing
A grand new collection for Sunday-schools, Christian endeavor, Epworth League, revival, camp and prayer meetings

ISBN/EAN: 9783337223502

Printed in Europe, USA, Canada, Australia, Japan

Cover: Foto ©Lupo / pixelio.de

More available books at **www.hansebooks.com**

Rich in Blessing

BY

GEO. C. HUGG.

A Grand New Collection for Sunday-Schools, Christian Endeavor, Epworth League, Revival, Camp and Prayer Meetings, Choirs, and the Home Circle.

$30.00 per Hundred. $3.60 per Dozen.
35 cents Singly.

Ward & Drummond,   George C. Hugg,
711 Broadway,   2133 Newkirk St.
New York.   Philadelphia.

Prefatory.

In the compilation of "Rich in Blessing" great care has been taken in selection of soul-stirring hymns, and the wedding of suitable music thereto. The author of said work has always had in mind the redeeming influences of God's word, and has endeavored to make a collection of songs capable of stirring up the souls of men, and leading them into the beautiful light of eternal day. This work will be a great helper in all active Christian work, and it is hoped that its influence may be felt for many years. Believing God's blessing will accompany the redeeming spirit of the songs herein contained, it is sent forward on its mission of blessing and gladness.

GEO. C. HUGG, Author.

Announcement.

Knowing that many church and sunday-school choristers, superintendents, and committees have acquired the pernicious habit of printing slips from copyright property, without first having obtained the legal right from the owner thereof, the author of "Rich in Blessing" wishes to state that his copyrights are his stock in trade, and that no one has any more right to appropriate said copyright property than his real estate or bank account; that having complied with all the requirements of the copyright law, he will stand under the protecting wings of said law, and bring to justice all offenders coming under his knowledge; therefore all persons are cautioned against writing, type writing, transferring, printing, or reproducing in any manner said copyright property, without first having been granted the permission in writing.

GEO. C. HUGG.

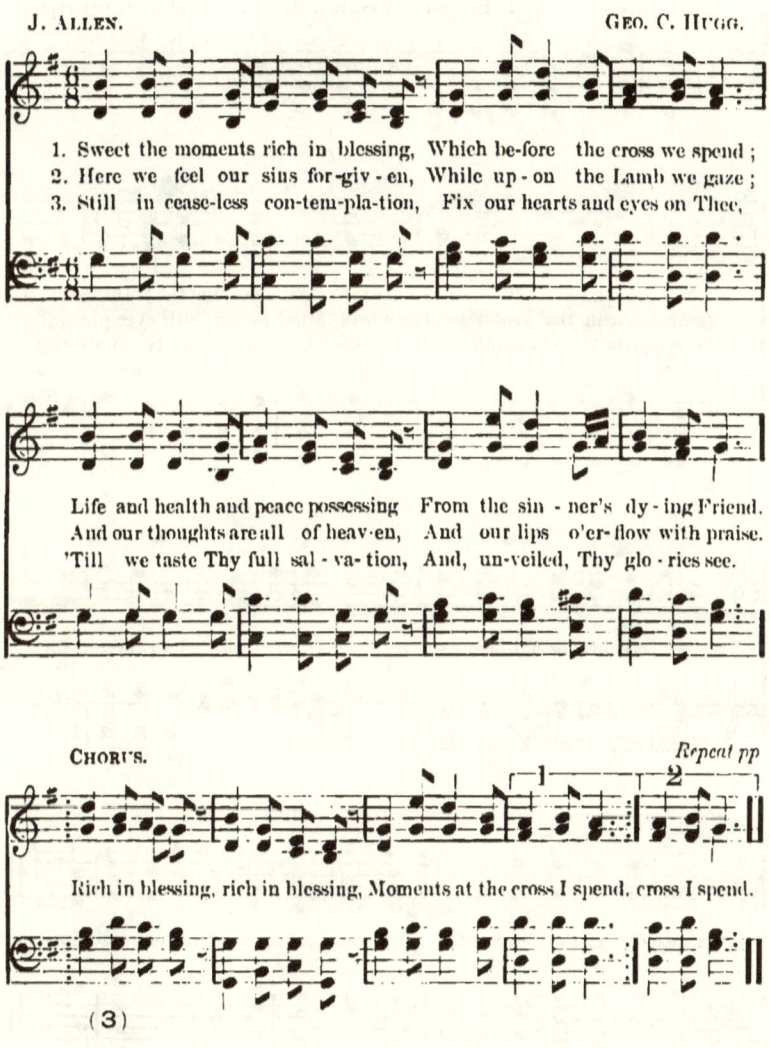

4 LAUNCH OUT.

Mrs. Rawl.   B. C. Unseld.

1. O fish-er-man toil-ing in shal-lows, And toiling all night in vain;
2. Launch out, for His hal-low-ed pres-ence Sus-tain-eth thy ves-sel frail;
3. Launch out with a faith un-wav-'ring, Returning with treasures replete,

E'er sein-ing in oft tried wa-ters, And shunning the path-less main.
Launch out in thy weakness—His power, Must ev-er, still ever pre-vail.
Bring pearls from the depths of the o-cean, As tro-phies to lay at **His** feet.

REFRAIN.

Launch out on the fath-om-less o-cean Of darkness and sorrow and sin;

Launch out at the word of the Mas-ter, And gath-er the out-casts in.

Copyright, 1893, by The Lutheran Publishing Society.

SATISFIED.

HORATIUS BONAR. GEO. C. HUGG.

1. When I awake in the sweet morn of morns, After whose dawning night ne'er returns:
2. When I shall meet with the ones I have lov'd, Clasp in my arms the long, long remov'd,
3. When I shall gaze on the dear face of Him, Who died for me, with eye no more dim,

And with whose glory the day ev-er burns, I shall be sat-is-fied.
And find how faithful the Lord then has proved, I shall be sat-is-fied.
And praise Him ever with heaven's swelling hymn, I shall be sat-is-fied.

CHORUS.

I shall be sat-is-fied; I shall be sat-is-fied;
I shall be satisfied, I shall be satisfied,

When in the like-ness of God I'm ar-rayed, I shall be sat-is-fied.

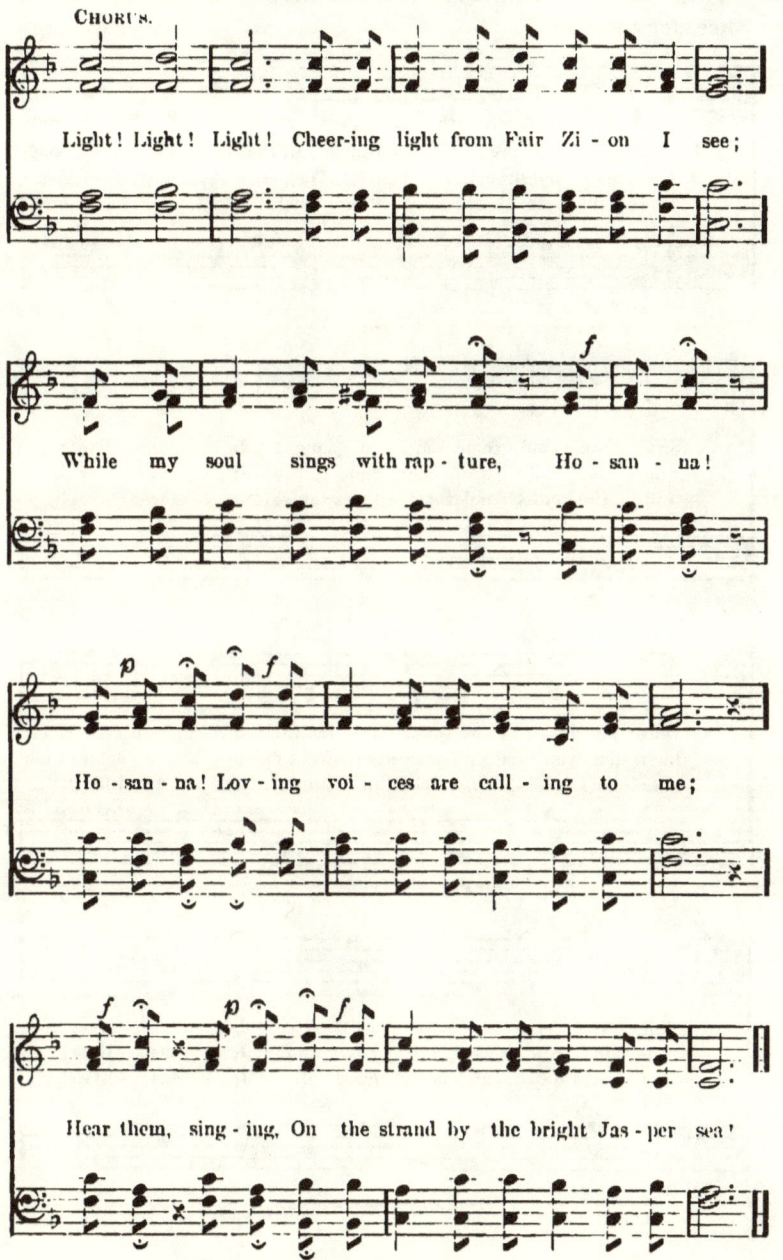

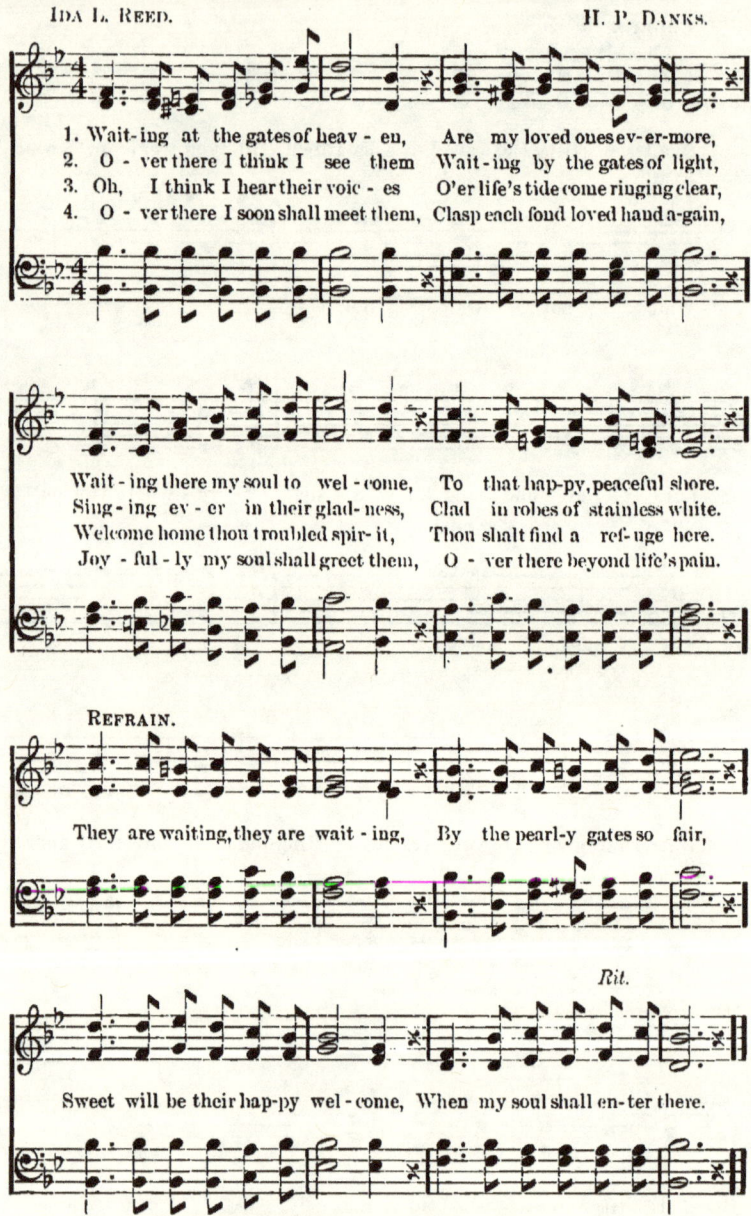

STEER TOWARD THE LIGHT.

15

GERTRUDE T. CLARK.
W. A. OGDEN.

1. Fierce is the tem-pest, loud is its roar, Storm-tossed the mar-in-er,
2. Storms can-not hide it, years can-not fade; Firm its foun-da-tion is,
3. When wild the tem-pest round thee is hurled, Look un-to Je-sus, the

far from the shore; See! what is put-ting the dark-ness to flight?
be not a-fraid; Heav'n's ample har-bor shall soon greet thy sight.
hope of the world; Bright shall the day be that fol-lows the night,

CHORUS.

Je-sus, the Morning Star, steer t'ward the light!
Watch for the dawn of day, steer t'ward the light! } Brightly it gleams, and its
Cour-age, then, mar-in-er, steer t'ward the light!

pure sil-ver beams Scat-ter the gloom of the night, of the night; Tho' the

f

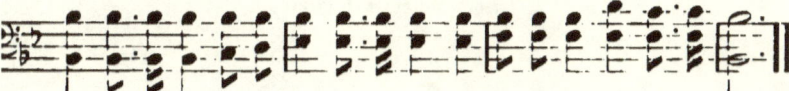

storms round thee rave, He is mighty to save, Then, mariner, steer t'ward the light

Copyright, 1891, by Chas. H. Gabriel.

IS THY CRUSE ALMOST EXHAUSTED? 17

Arr. from Mrs. E. R. CHARLES. D. C. JOHN.

1. Is thy cruse al-most ex-haust-ed? Share it still with needy friend,
2. Human hearts grow rich in giv - ing, For true wealth is liv-ing grain;
3. Is thy heart a well left emp - ty? None but God its void can fill;

And thro' all the years of fam - ine It shall last thee to the end;
Seeds which molder in the gar - ner, Scattered, clothe the gold-en plain;
Nothing but a ceaseless fount - ain Can its cease - less longing still;

For the Lord will mul-ti-ply it, And thy hand - ful still re - new;
Is thy bur - den ver - y heav - y? Art thou temp - ted to re - pine?
Is thy heart a liv-ing pow - er? Self-absorbed its strength sinks low;

Scant-y fare for one will oft - en Make a roy - al feast for two,
Help to lift thy wea - ry broth-er's, And the Lord will light-en thine,
It can live by lov-ing on - ly, And by serv - ing love will grow.

Scant-y fare for one will oft - en Make a roy - al feast for two,
Help to lift thy wea - ry broth-er's, And the Lord will lighten thine,
It can live by lov-ing on - ly, And by serv - ing love will grow.

Copyright, 1891, by D. C. John.

IN THE HAPPY LAND.

E. E. Hewitt.   Geo. C. Hugg.

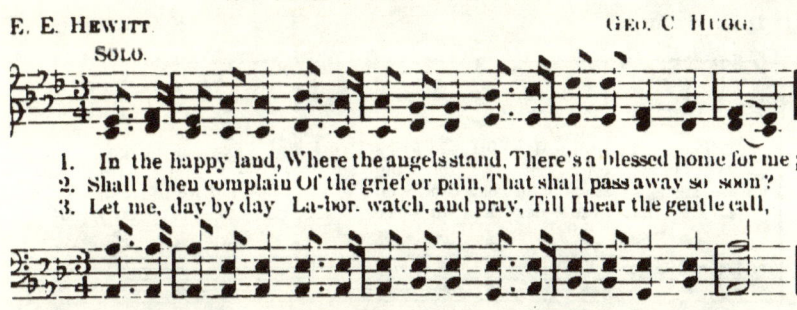

1. In the happy land, Where the angels stand, There's a blessed home for me;
2. Shall I then complain Of the grief or pain, That shall pass away so soon?
3. Let me, day by day Labor, watch, and pray, Till I hear the gentle call,

For a mansion fair, Will the Lord prepare; There His glorious face I'll see.
When the shadows flee, And the light I see Of the bright, e-ter-nal noon
"Come, ye blessed, come, To the blood-bought home, Just beyond the jasper-wall"

CHORUS.

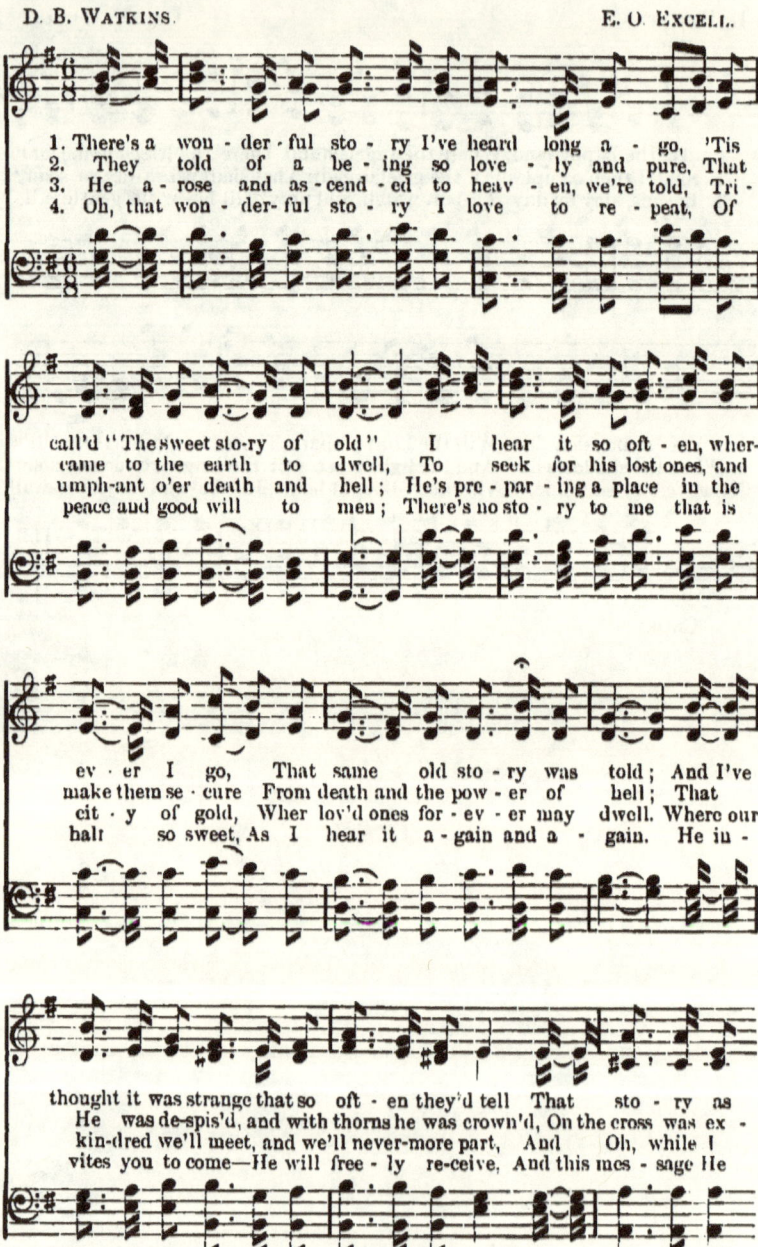

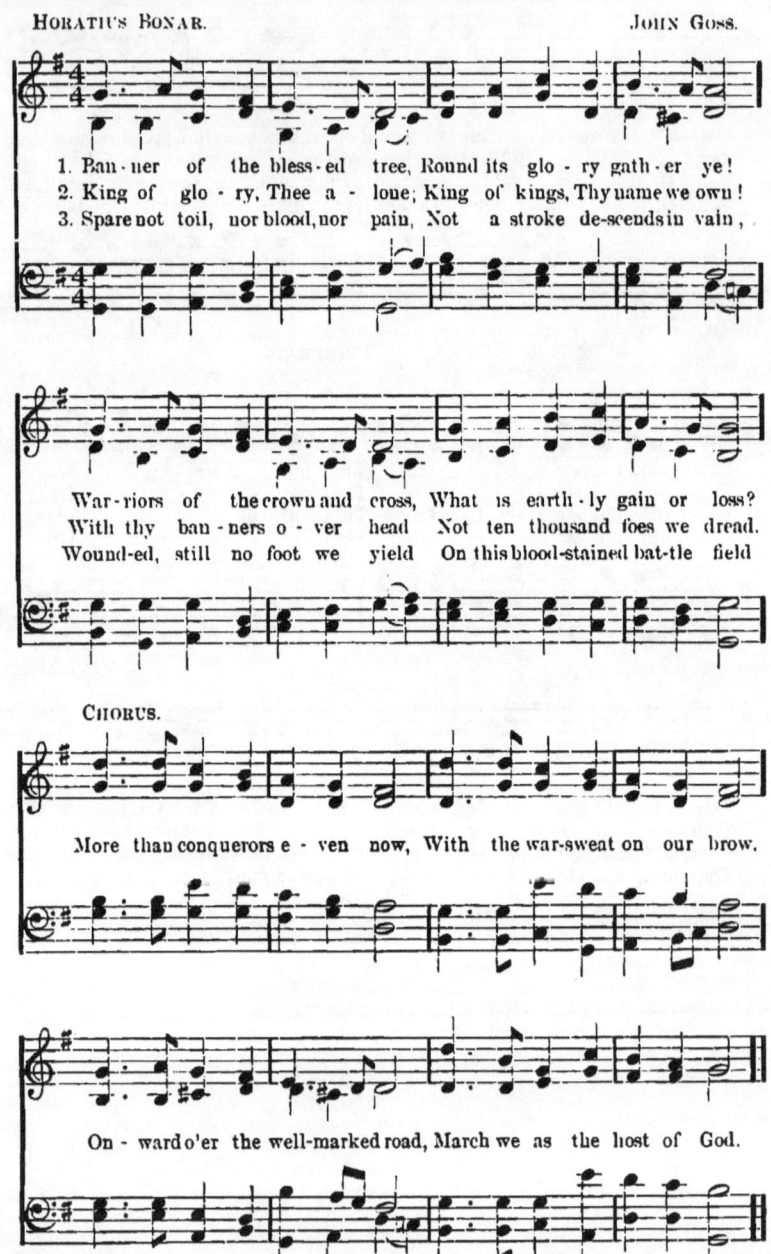

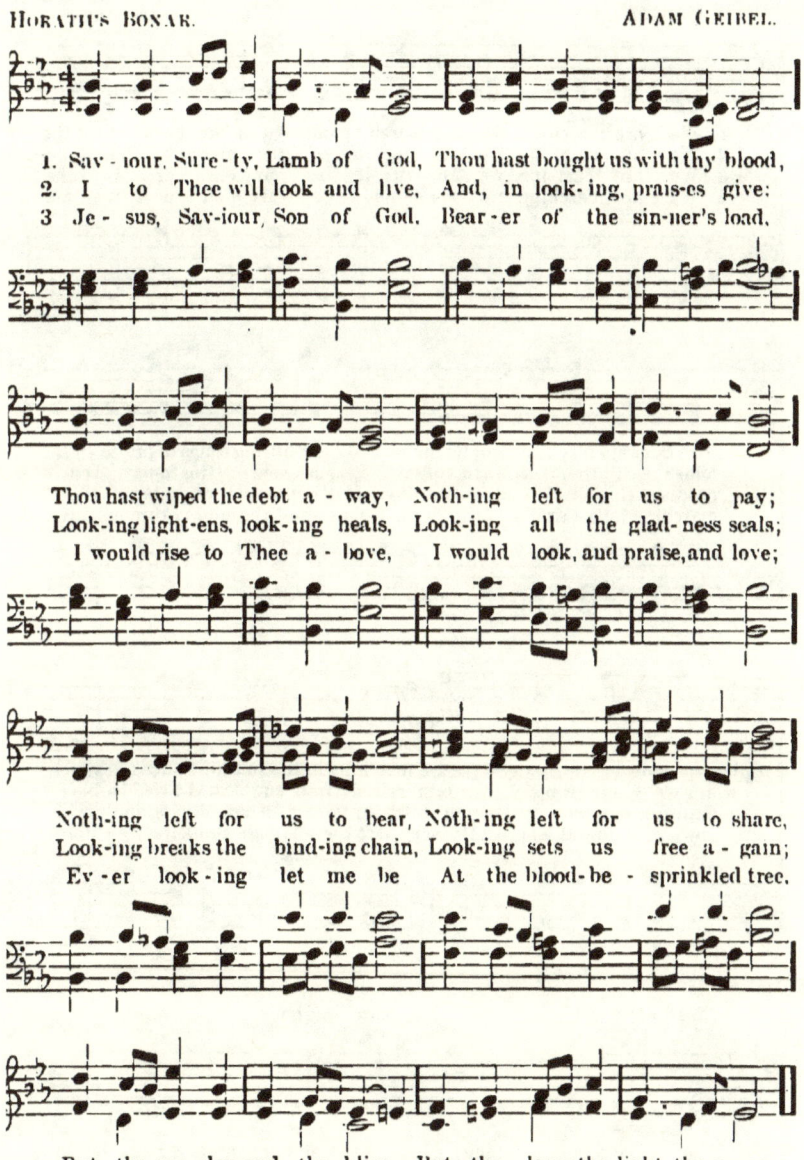

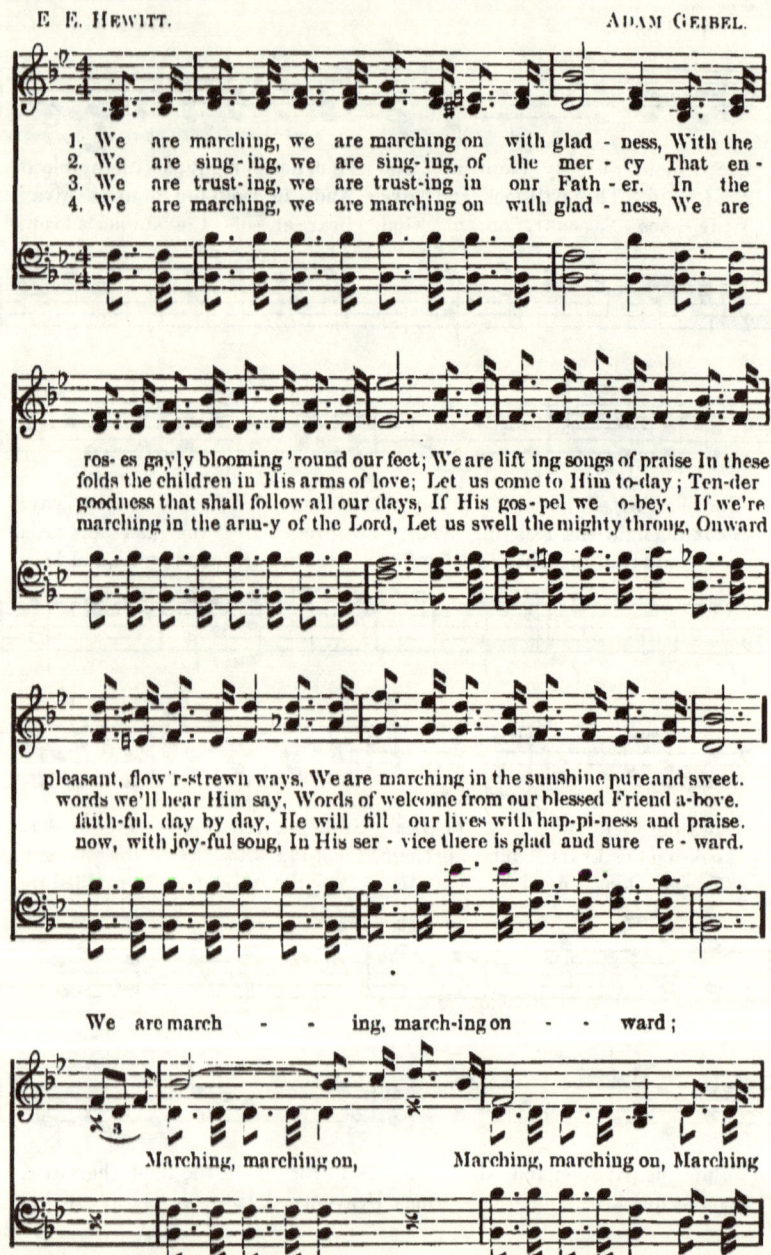

MARCHING ON WITH GLADNESS. Concluded.

marching on with shout and song; In the sunshine, pure and sweet, With the

ros - es 'round our feet, We are marching on, a glad, re-joic - ing throng.

DUNDEE.

J. ADDISON. G. FRANC.

1. When all thy mer-cies, O my God, My ris - ing soul sur-veys,
2. O how can words with e - qual warmth The grat-i - tude de - clare,
3. When in the slip - p'ry paths of youth, With heedless steps I ran,
4. Through ev-'ry pe - riod of my life Thy good - ness I'll pur - sue;

Trans-port - ed with the view, I'm lost In won-der, love, and praise.
That glows with-in my rav - ished heart? But thou canst read it there.
Thine arm, un - seen, con-veyed me safe, And led me up to man.
And af - ter death, in dis - tant worlds, The pleas-ing theme re - new.

TRUST IN THE LORD WITH ALL THINE HEART. 33

E. E. HEWITT.   ADAM GEIBEL.

1. Trust in the Lord with all thine heart, Hope from His mercy bor - row;
2. On Him, with child-like faith repose, In ev - 'ry hour of sad - ness;
3. Why should we doubt our Father's love? So warm, so deep, and tender,
4. Trust in the Lord with all thine heart; A-way with all mis - giv - ing!

His kindness nev-er will de-part, The same to - day, to - mor - row.
His might-y arms a-round thee close, He'll give thee songs of glad-ness.
O let us lift our eyes a-bove, And ev - 'ry fear sur - ren - der.
The light will come, the clouds depart, For Je-sus, still is liv - ing,

CHORUS.
Trust   in the Lord;

Trust, trust; trust in the Lord; The light will come; the clouds depart;

Trust,   in the Lord;

trust, trust, trust in the Lord; Trust in the Lord with all thine heart.

WORK FOR JESUS EVERYWHERE. Concluded. 35

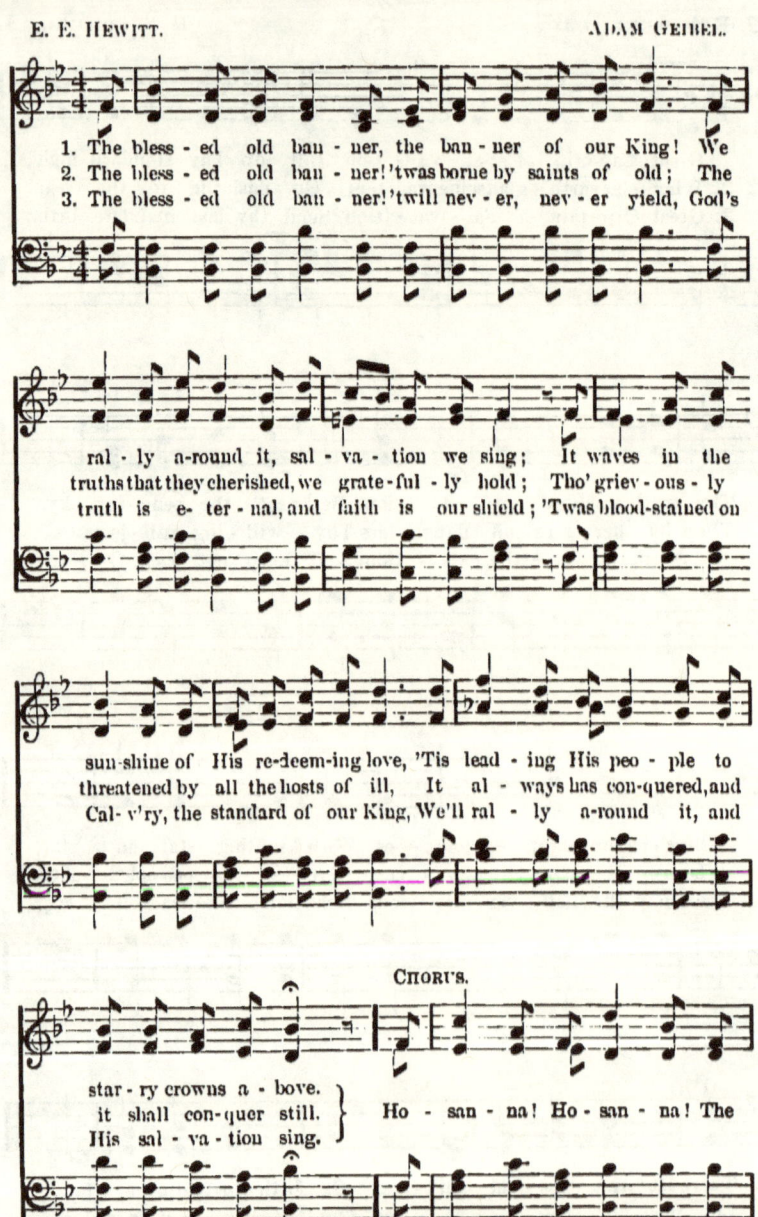

THE BLESSED OLD BANNER. Concluded. 39

bless - ed old ban - ner, The ban-ner of the cross we bear,

Ho - san - na! Ho - san - na! The bless - ed old ban - ner;

We'll bear it for the Mas - ter, till in His joy we share.

BLEST BE THE TIE.

JOHN FAWCETT.   GEO. NAEGELI.

4. Yes, blessed Jesus, yes, I may
Go work for Thee throughout this day,
And all the joy or good I crave,
Is but some fallen soul to save.

5. I'll work for Thee, Thou blessed One,
Eternal God, eternal Son,
And boast, but never boast in vain,
I'll work for Him who once was slain.

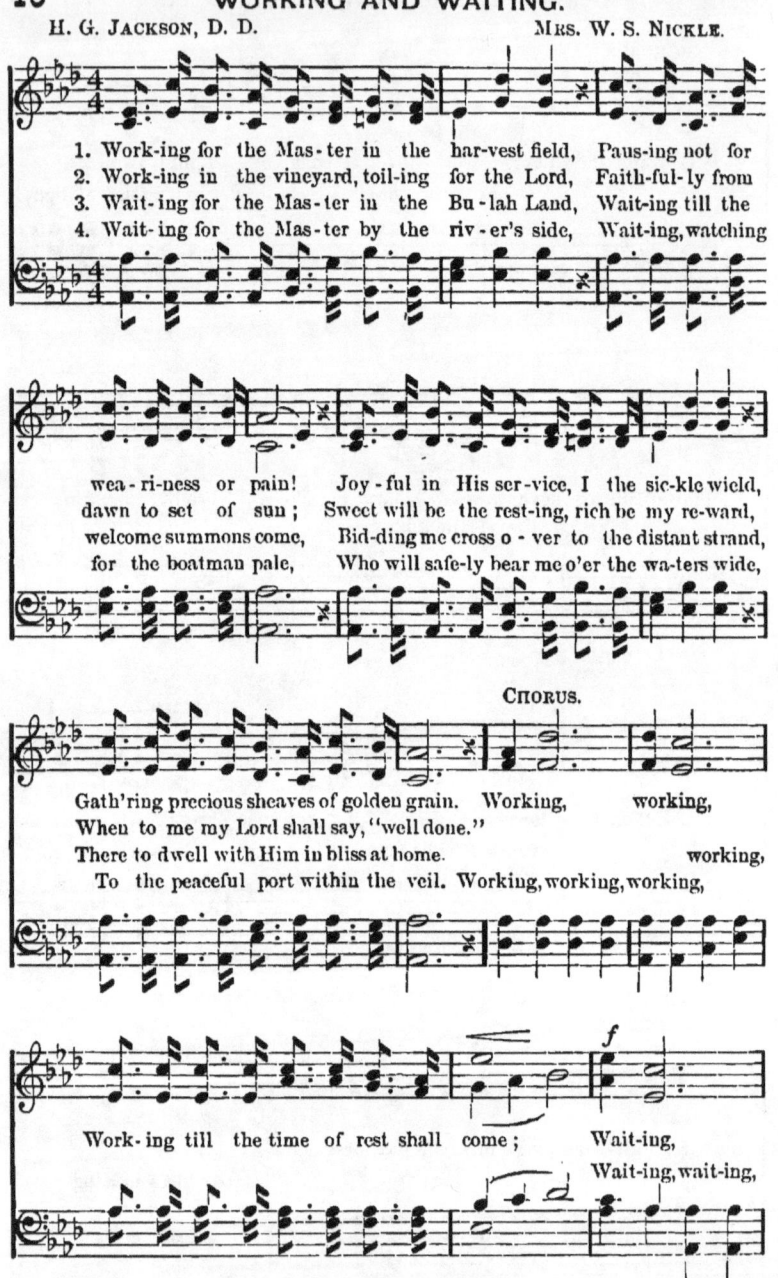

WORKING AND WAITING. Concluded. 47

wait-ing, Wait-ing till the Lord shall call me home.
wait-ing, wait-ing,

ALL HAIL THE POWER OF JESUS' NAME.

REV. E. PERRONET.   O. HOLDEN.

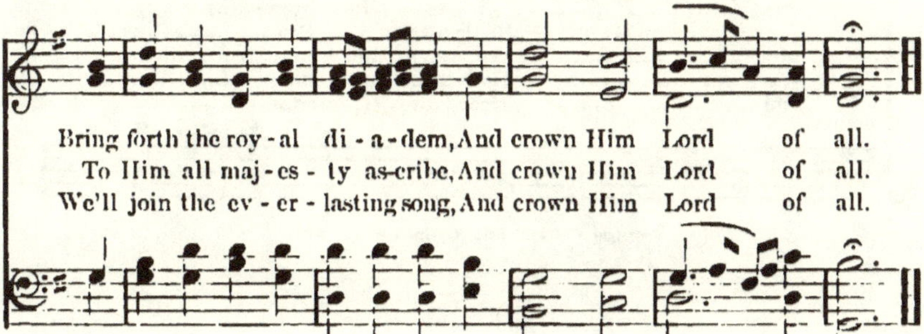

1. All hail the pow'r of Je - sus' name! Let an - gels pros-trate fall;
2. Let ev - 'ry kin - dred, ev - 'ry tribe, On this ter - res - trial ball,
3. Oh, that with yon - der sa - cred throng, We at His feet may fall;

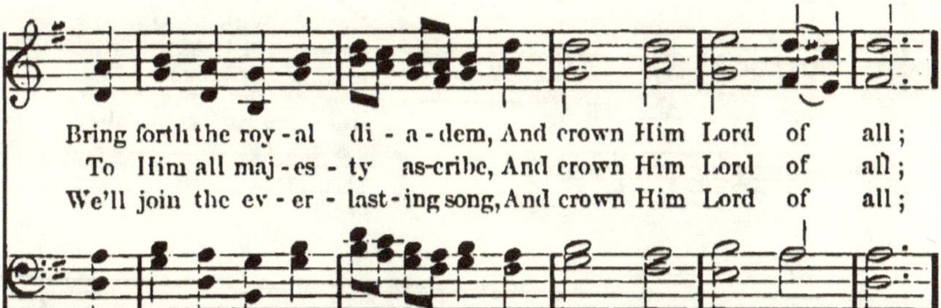

Bring forth the roy - al di - a - dem, And crown Him Lord of all;
To Him all maj - es - ty as-cribe, And crown Him Lord of all;
We'll join the ev - er - last-ing song, And crown Him Lord of all;

Bring forth the roy - al di - a - dem, And crown Him Lord of all.
To Him all maj - es - ty as-cribe, And crown Him Lord of all.
We'll join the ev - er - lasting song, And crown Him Lord of all.

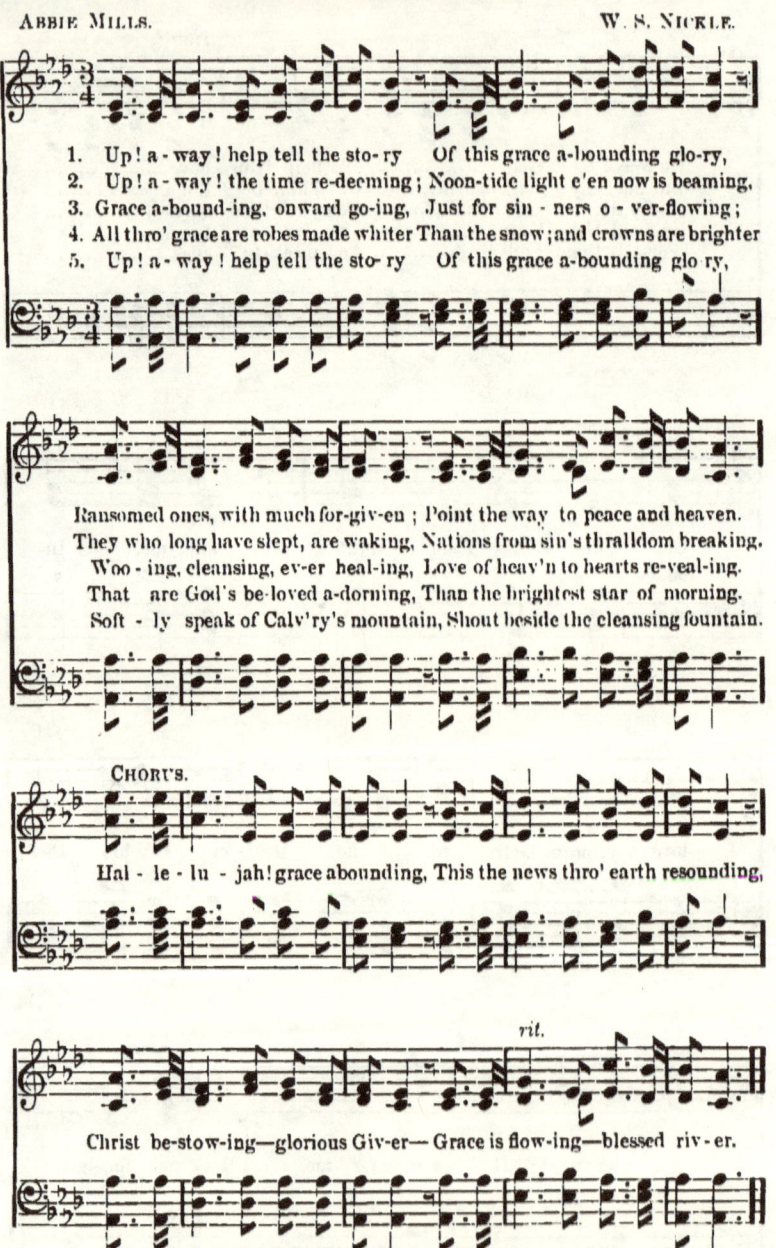

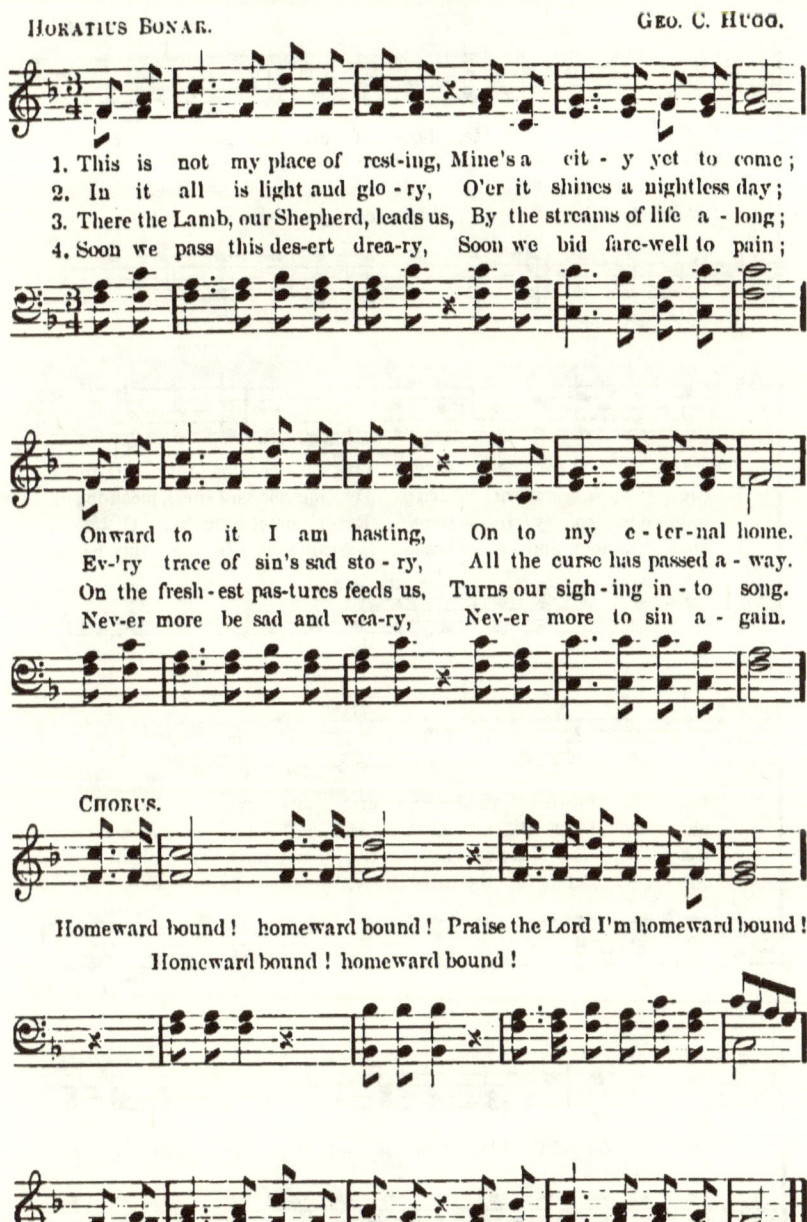

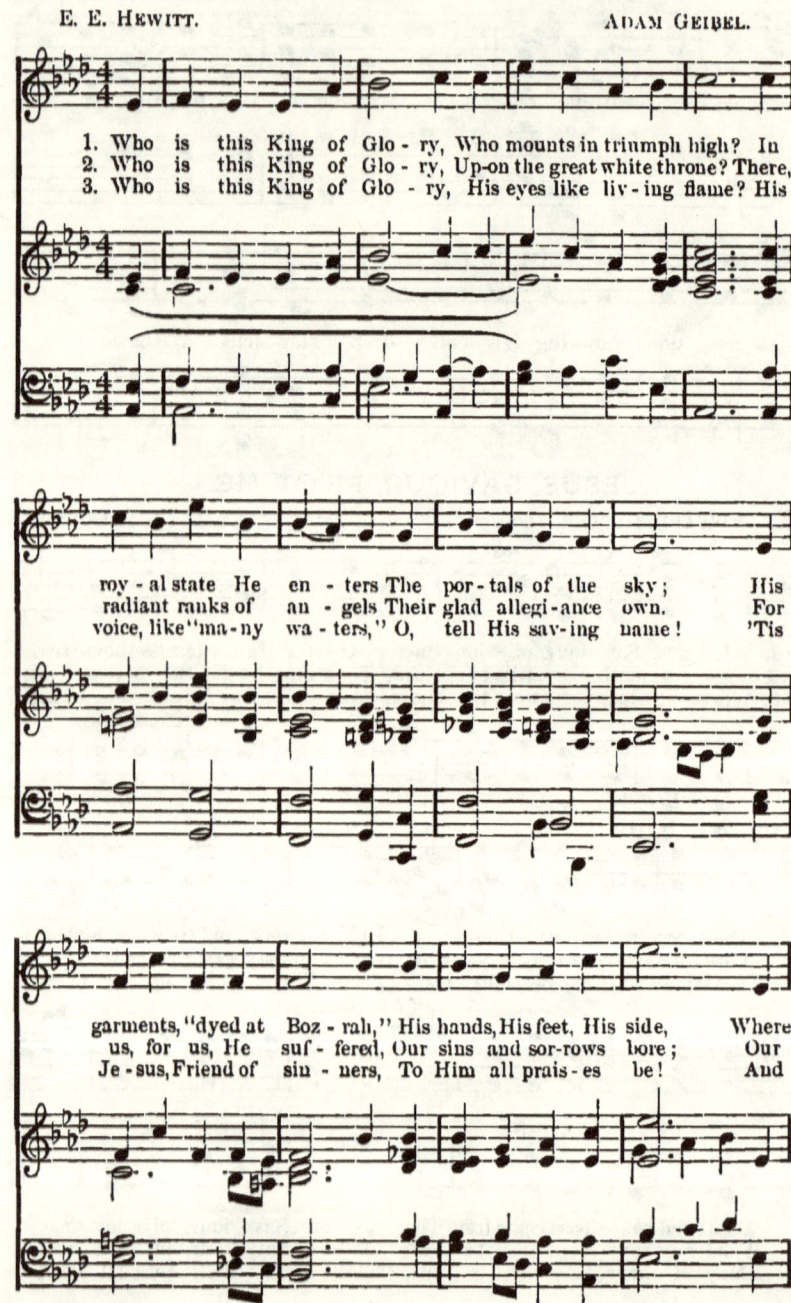

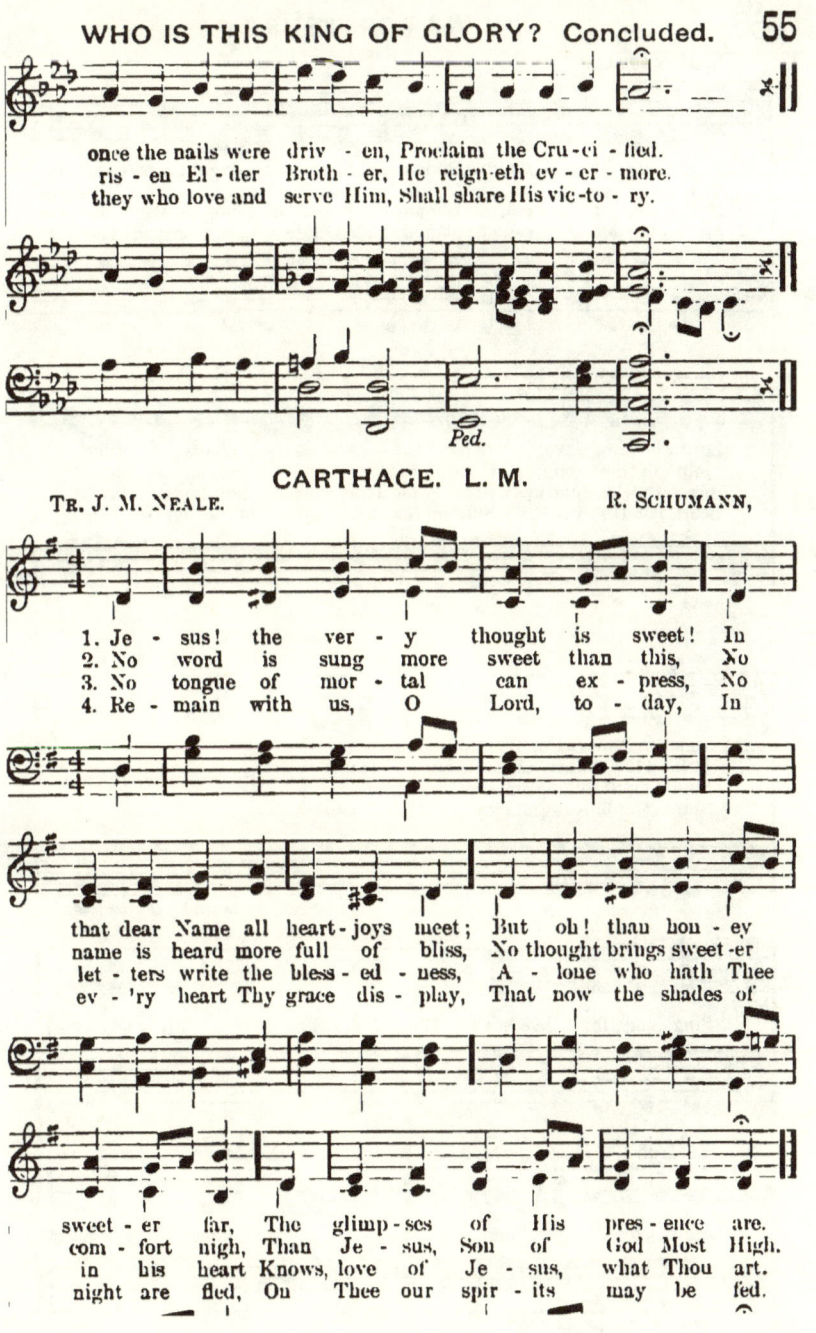

NOT A MOUNTAIN STREAMLET.

E. E. Hewitt. Adam Geibel.

1. Not a mountain streamlet, Singing as it flows, But the way before it, God our Father knows. Not a star that circles In the midnight sky, But is 'neath the guiding Of His watchful eye.
2. Not a little sparrow Flutters to the ground, Not a hungry robin In the forest found, But our Father seeth, Careth for their need, Not a cry of sorrow, But His ear takes heed.
3. Not a contrite spirit, Seeking for relief Comes in faith to Jesus, With its load of grief, But His voice so tender, Whispers peace within, And His blood, so precious, Cleanseth from all sin.

CHORUS.

Not a life too lowly, For the Father's care,
Not a heart too lonely, In His love to share.

PLANTING A BLESSING.

E. E. Hewitt.   Adam Geibel.

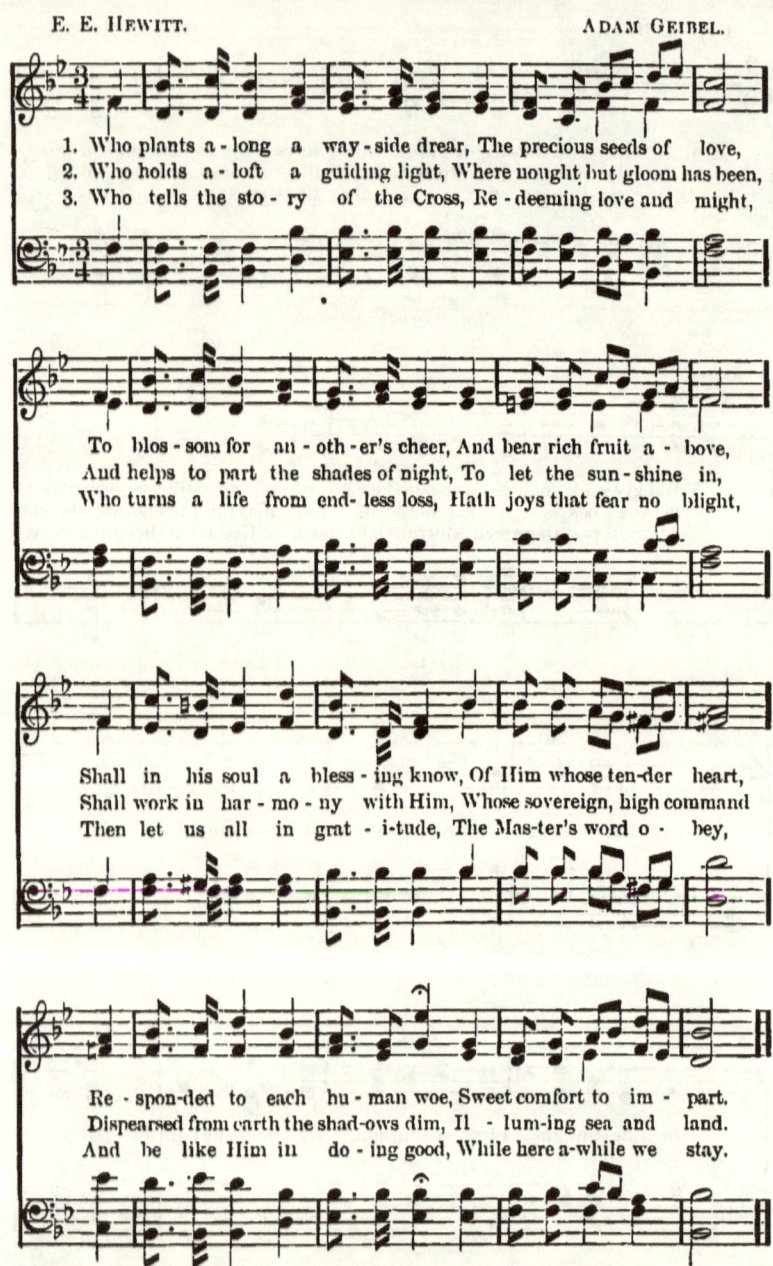

1. Who plants a-long a way-side drear, The precious seeds of love,
To blos-som for an-oth-er's cheer, And bear rich fruit a-bove,
Shall in his soul a bless-ing know, Of Him whose ten-der heart,
Re-spond-ed to each hu-man woe, Sweet comfort to im-part.

2. Who holds a-loft a guiding light, Where nought but gloom has been,
And helps to part the shades of night, To let the sun-shine in,
Shall work in har-mo-ny with Him, Whose sovereign, high command
Dispearsed from earth the shad-ows dim, Il-lum-ing sea and land.

3. Who tells the sto-ry of the Cross, Re-deeming love and might,
Who turns a life from end-less loss, Hath joys that fear no blight,
Then let us all in grat-i-tude, The Mas-ter's word o-bey,
And be like Him in do-ing good, While here a-while we stay.

WAIT PATIENTLY.

F. R. HAVERGAL. *Moderato.*   GEO. C. HUGG.

1. God doth not bid thee wait, To dis-ap-point at last;
2. The wear-y wait-ing times, Are but the muf-fled peals:
3. He doth not bid thee wait, Like drift-wood on the wave,

A gol-den prom-ise fair and great In pre-cept mould is cast,
Low pre-lud-ing ce - les-tial chimes, That hail His char-iot wheels,
For fic-kle chance, or fix-ed fate, To ru-in or to save,

Soon shall the morn-ing gild The dark ho-ri-zon rim,
Trust Him to tune thy voice, To blend with ser-a-phim;
Thine eyes shall sure-ly see, No dist-ant hope or dim,

Thy heart's de-sire shall be ful-filled, Wait pa-tient-ly for Him.
His wait shall is-sue in re-joice, Wait pa-tient-ly for Him.
The Lord thy God a-rose for thee, Wait pa-tient-ly for Him.

ff CHORUS. *Slow.*   *pp*

Wait pa-tient-ly for Him! Wait pa-tient-ly for Him!

BRIGHTLY GLEAMS OUR BANNER. Concluded.

Still, with hearts u - nit - ed, Sing - ing on our way.
Keep us, might - y Sav - iour, In the nar - row way.
Save to Thee, our Sav - iour, On - ly un - to Thee?
Par - don Thou and save us In the last dread hour.

f Chorus.

Bright-ly gleams our ban - ner, Point-ing to the sky,

Ped.

Unison.

Wav - ing wand'rers on - ward To their home on high. A - men.

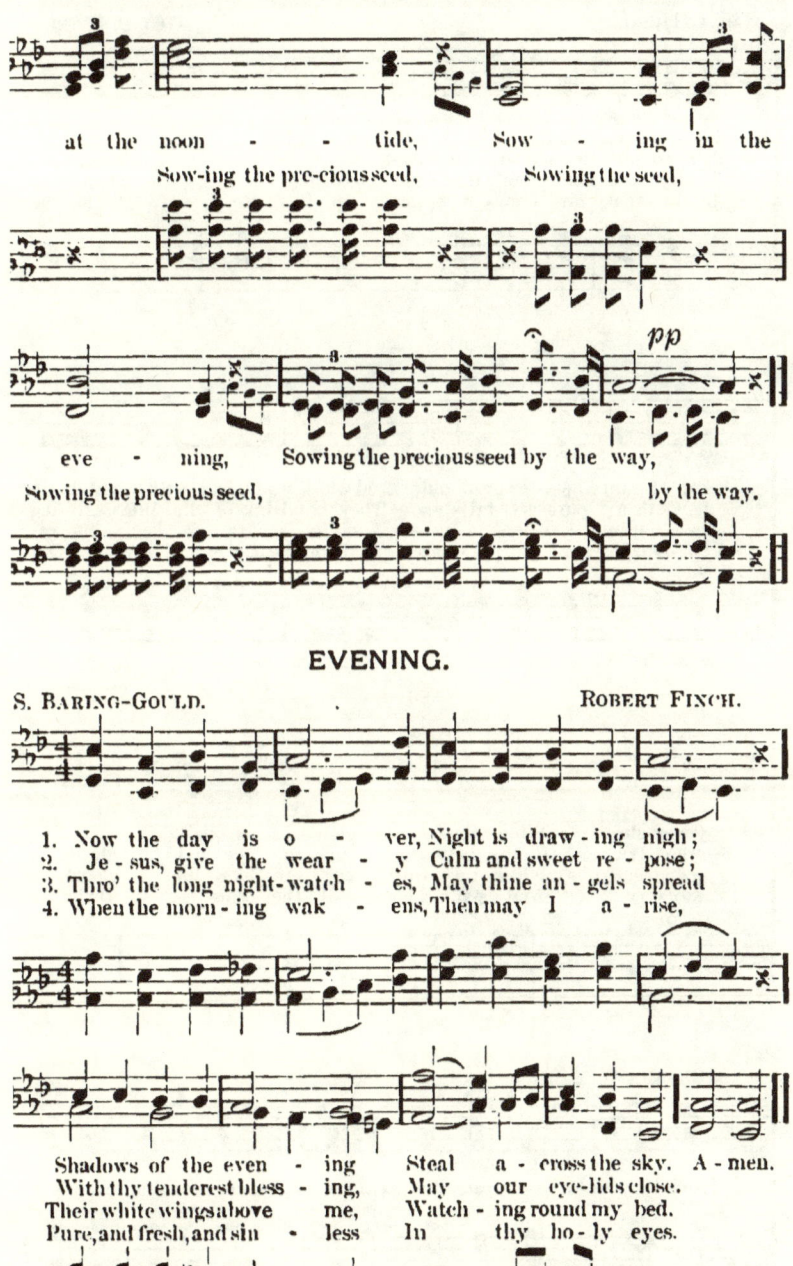

NO CANDLE, NOR SUN. Concluded.

SUN OF MY SOUL.

J. KEBLE.   W. H. MONK.

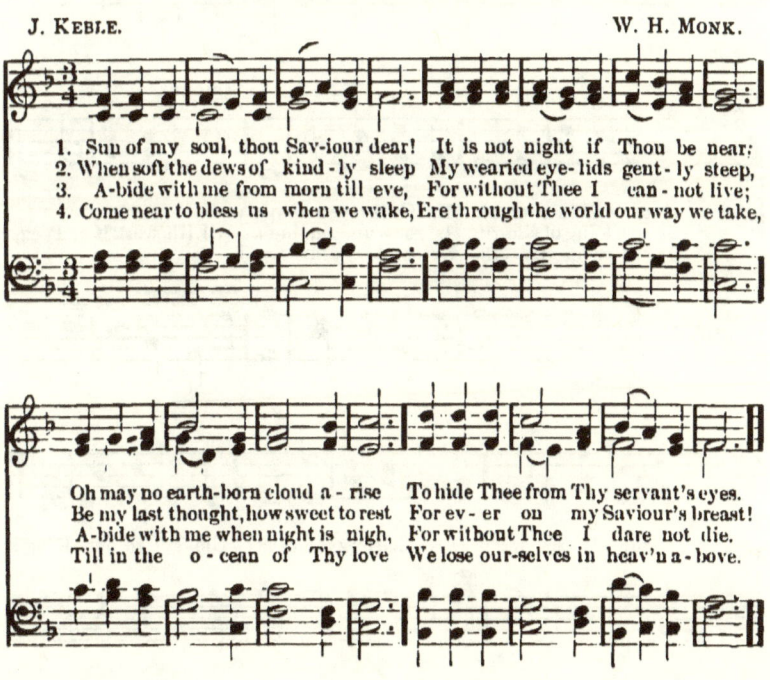

THE WORKER'S PRAYER. 77

F. R. Havergal.
Geo. C. Hugg.

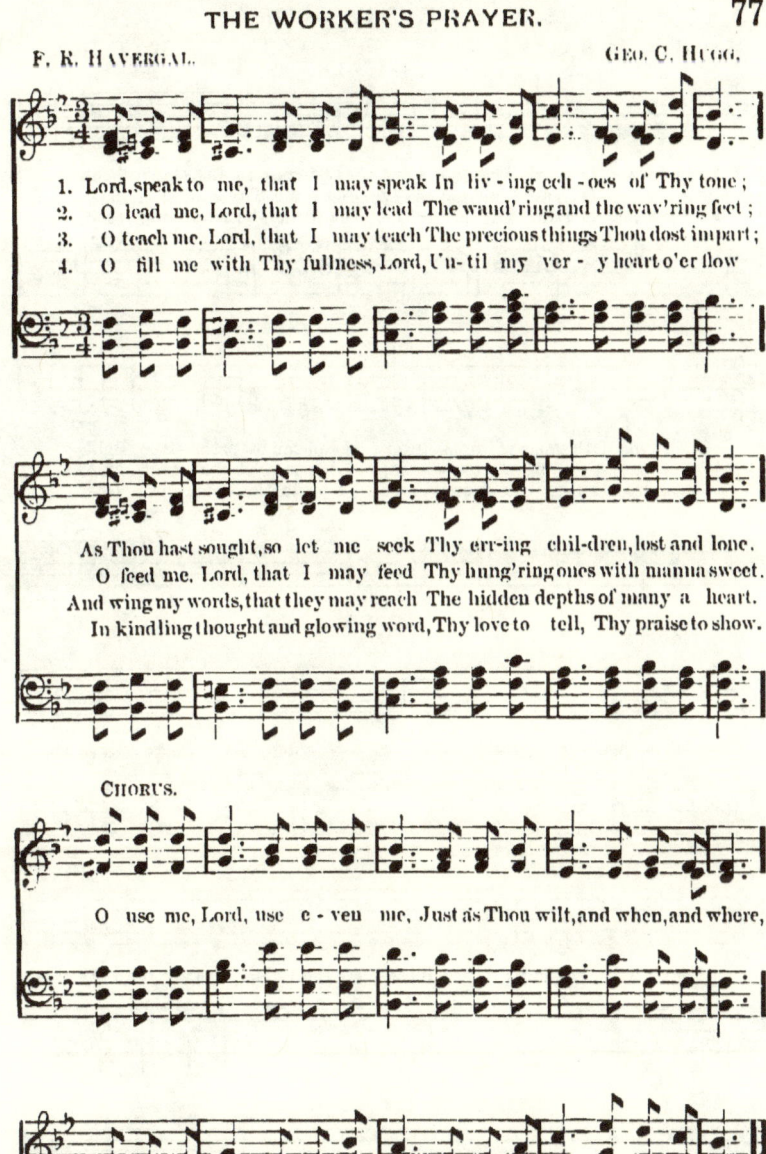

1. Lord, speak to me, that I may speak In liv-ing ech-oes of Thy tone;
2. O lead me, Lord, that I may lead The wand'ring and the wav'ring feet;
3. O teach me, Lord, that I may teach The precious things Thou dost impart;
4. O fill me with Thy fullness, Lord, Un-til my ver-y heart o'er flow

As Thou hast sought, so let me seek Thy err-ing chil-dren, lost and lone.
O feed me, Lord, that I may feed Thy hung'ring ones with manna sweet.
And wing my words, that they may reach The hidden depths of many a heart.
In kindling thought and glowing word, Thy love to tell, Thy praise to show.

CHORUS.

O use me, Lord, use e-ven me, Just as Thou wilt, and when, and where,

Un-til Thy bless-ed face I see, Thy rest, Thy joy, Thy glo-ry share.

SHOW ME THY GLORY.

Mrs. Harriet E. Jones.
Geo. C. Hugg.

With feeling.

1. Show me, O Lord, Thy glo - ry, Lift me to Beu-lah's height,
2. Show me, O Lord, Thy glo - ry, Show me Thy smil-ing face;
3. Show me, O Lord, Thy glo - ry, Show me the shin-ing road,

Fill me with songs of rapt - ure, Lead me in paths of light.
Give me a glimpse of Ca - naan, Give me rich show'rs of grace.
Lead me, O dear Re-deem - er, Up to the home of God.

CHORUS.

O - pen the gates of E - den, Show me the heav'n - ly place; Bless - ed the vis - ions of beau - ty un - fold - ing, O, show me Thy smil - ing face.

BEYOND.

ORATIUS BONAR. GEO. C. HUGG.

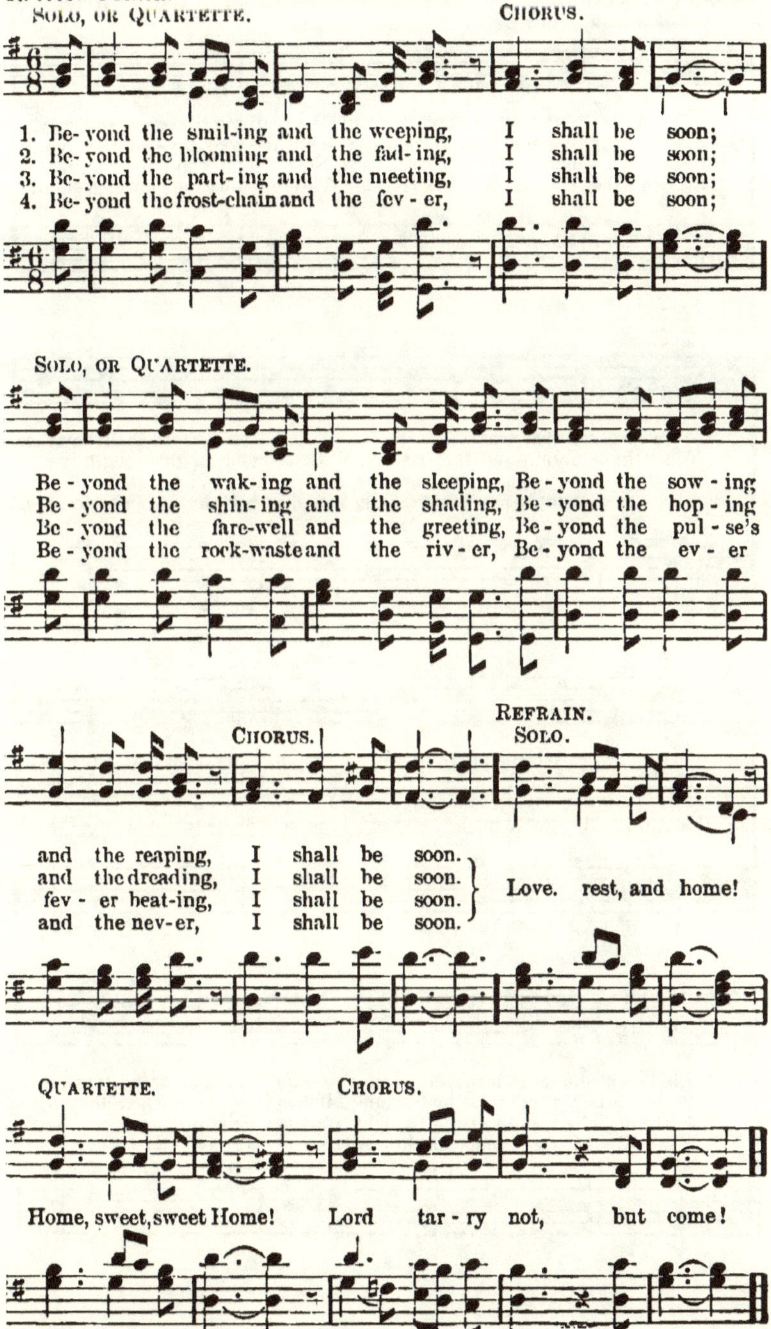
SOLO, OR QUARTETTE.
CHORUS.
1. Be-yond the smil-ing and the weeping, I shall be soon;
2. Be-yond the blooming and the fad-ing, I shall be soon;
3. Be-yond the part-ing and the meeting, I shall be soon;
4. Be-yond the frost-chain and the fev-er, I shall be soon;
SOLO, OR QUARTETTE.
Be-yond the wak-ing and the sleeping, Be-yond the sow-ing
Be-yond the shin-ing and the shading, Be-yond the hop-ing
Be-yond the fare-well and the greeting, Be-yond the pul-se's
Be-yond the rock-waste and the riv-er, Be-yond the ev-er
CHORUS.
REFRAIN.
SOLO.
and the reaping, I shall be soon.
and the dreading, I shall be soon.
fev-er beat-ing, I shall be soon.
and the nev-er, I shall be soon.
Love. rest, and home!
QUARTETTE.
CHORUS.
Home, sweet, sweet Home! Lord tar-ry not, but come!

* This composition may be sung as Chorus throughout.

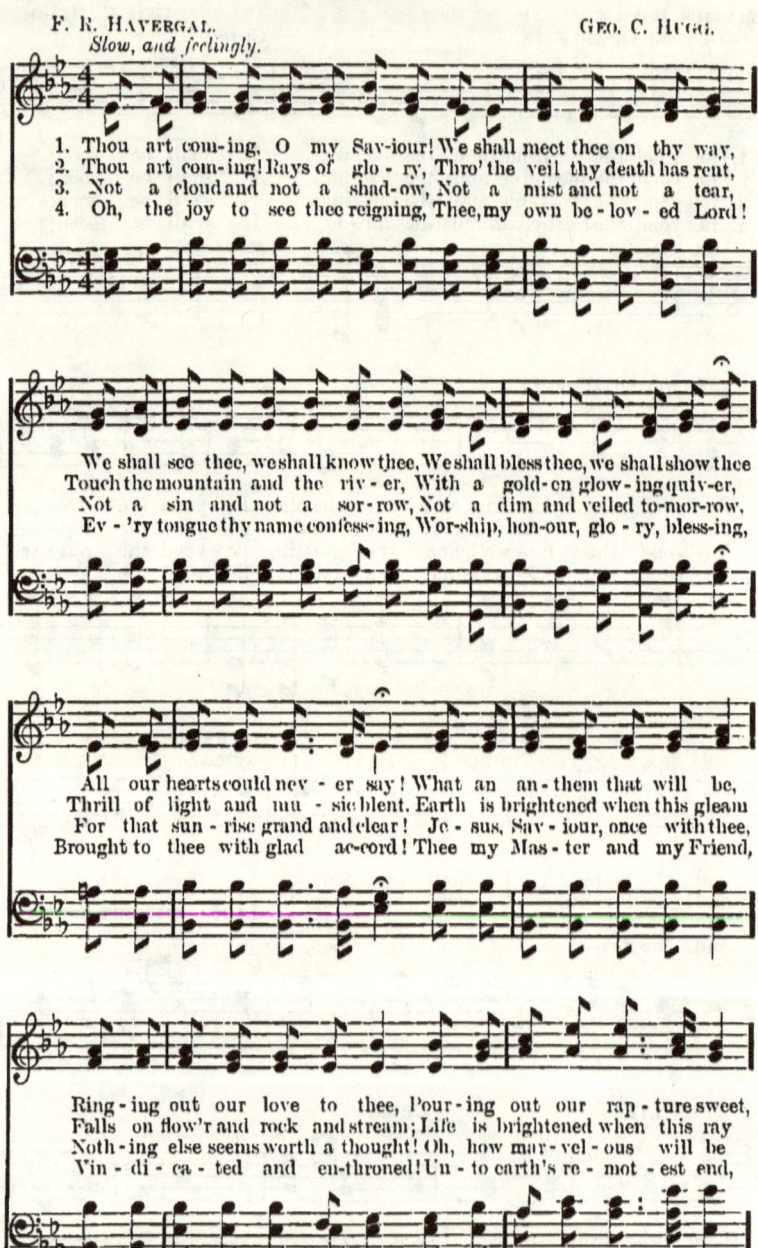

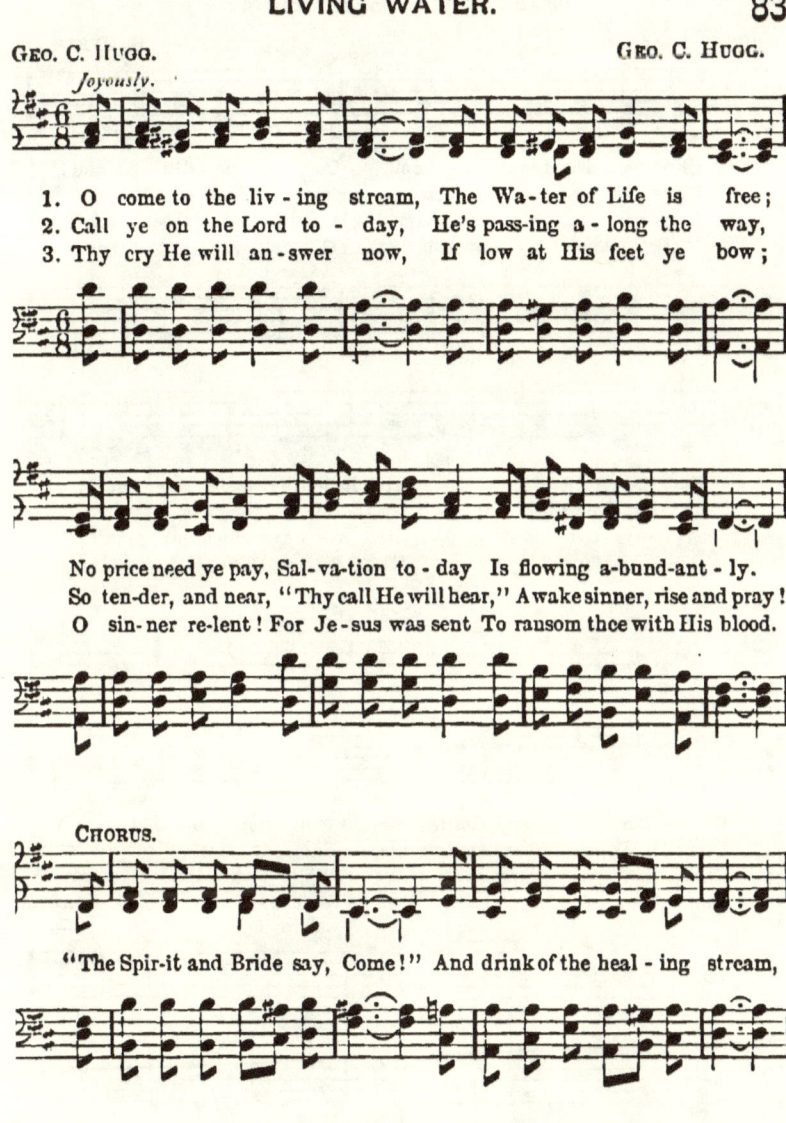

AT LAST! Concluded. 87

On the Jasper threshold standing,
Like a pilgrim safely landing,
See, the strange bright scene expanding,
    Ah! 'tis heaven at last!—Cho.

What a city! what a glory
Far beyond the brightest story,
Of the ages old and hoary;
    Ah! 'tis heaven at last!—Cho.

Softest voices, silver-pealing,
Freshest fragrance, spirit-healing,
Happy hymns around us stealing;
    Ah! 'tis heaven at last!—Cho.

Not a broken blossom yonder,
Not a link can snap asunder,   [der;
Stayed the tempest, sheathed the thun-
    Ah! 'tis heaven at last!—Cho.

7 Not a tear-drop ever falleth,
  Not a pleasure ever palleth,
  Song to song forever calleth;
    Ah! 'tis heaven at last!—Cho.

8 Christ himself the living splendour,
  Christ the sunlight mild and tender,
  Praises to the Lamb we render;
    Ah! 'tis heaven at last!—Cho.

9 Now at length the veil is rended,
  Now the pilgrimage is ended,
  And the Saints their thrones ascended;
    Ah! 'tis heaven at last!—Cho.

10 Broken death's dread bands that
    bound us,
   Life and victory around us;   [us;
   Christ, the King, himself hath crowned
    Ah! 'tis heaven at last!—Cho.

TRUTH DIVINE.

SAMUEL LONGFELLOW.   ROBERT FINCH.

1. Ho-ly Spir-it, Truth di-vine! Dawn up-on this soul of mine;
2. Ho-ly Spir-it, Love di-vine! Glow within this heart of mine;
3. Ho-ly Spir-it, Pow'r di-vine! Fill and nerve this will of mine;
4. Ho-ly Spir-it, Right di-vine! King within my conscience reign;

Word of God, and in-ward Light! Wake my spir-it, clear my sight.
Kin-dle ev-'ry high de-sire; Per-ish self in thy pure fire.
By thee may I strong-ly live, Brave-ly bear, and no-bly strive.
Be my law, and I shall be Firm-ly bound, for-ev-er free.

HAVE YOU NOT A WORD.

F. R. HAVERGAL.
Joyously.
GEO. C. HUGG.

1. Have you not a word for Je - sus? Not a word to say for Him?
2. He has spoken words of bless - ing, Pardon, peace, and love to you,
3. Have you not a word for Je - sus? Will the world His praise proclaim?
4. Have you not a word for Je - sus? Some, perchance while ye are dumb,

He is listening thro' the cho - rus Of the burning Ser - a - phim!
Glorious hope and gracious com - fort, Strong and tender, sweet and true;
Who will speak if ye are si - lent? Ye who know and love His name.
Wait and weary for your mes - sage, Hop - ing you will bid them come,

He is listening; does He hear you Speak-ing of the things of earth,
Does He hear you telling oth - ers Something of His love un - told,
You, whom He hath called and chosen His own wit - nesses to be,
Nev - er telling hidden sor - rows, Lingering just outside the door,

On - ly of its passing pleas - ure, Self - ish sorrow, empty mirth?
O - ver-flowings of thanksgiv - ing For His mercies man - i - fold?
Will you tell your gracious Mas - ter, Lord we cannot speak for Thee.
Longing for your hand to lead them In - to rest for ev - er-more.

SONGS OF LOVE. Concluded.

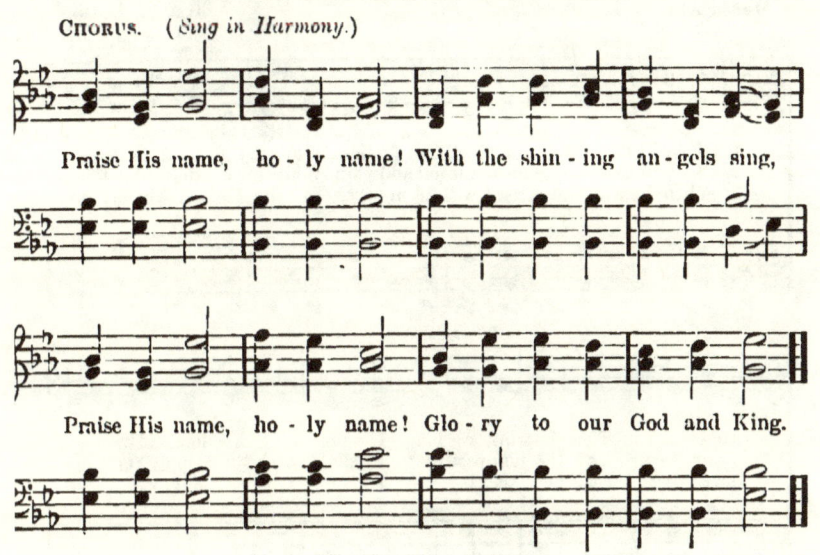

LIGHT OF DAY.

GEO. W. DOANE.   JOSEPH BARNBY.
p Slow.

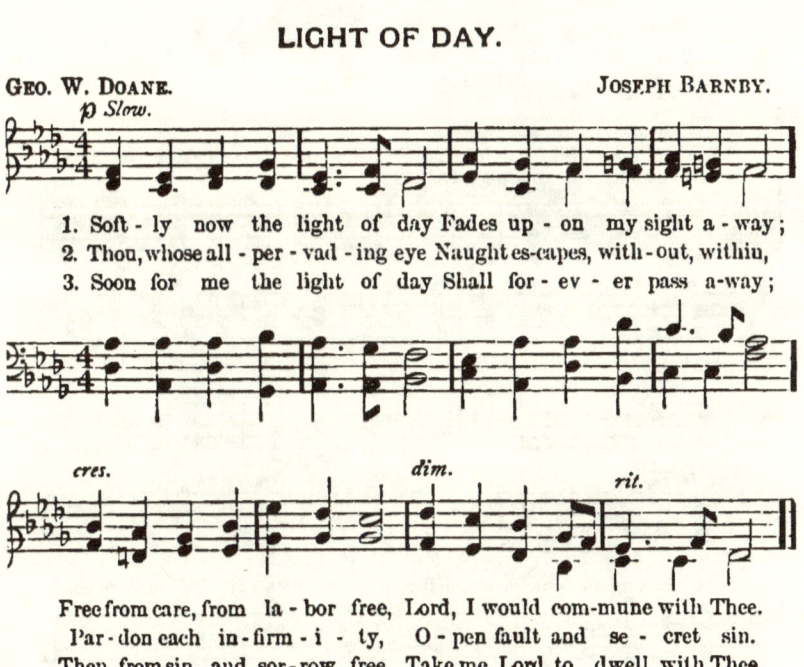

1. Soft-ly now the light of day Fades up-on my sight a-way;
2. Thou, whose all-per-vad-ing eye Naught es-capes, with-out, within,
3. Soon for me the light of day Shall for-ev-er pass a-way;

Free from care, from la-bor free, Lord, I would com-mune with Thee.
Par-don each in-firm-i-ty, O-pen fault and se-cret sin.
Then, from sin and sor-row free, Take me, Lord, to dwell with Thee.

HUMILITY.

93

D. CARLYLE.
J. B. DYKES.

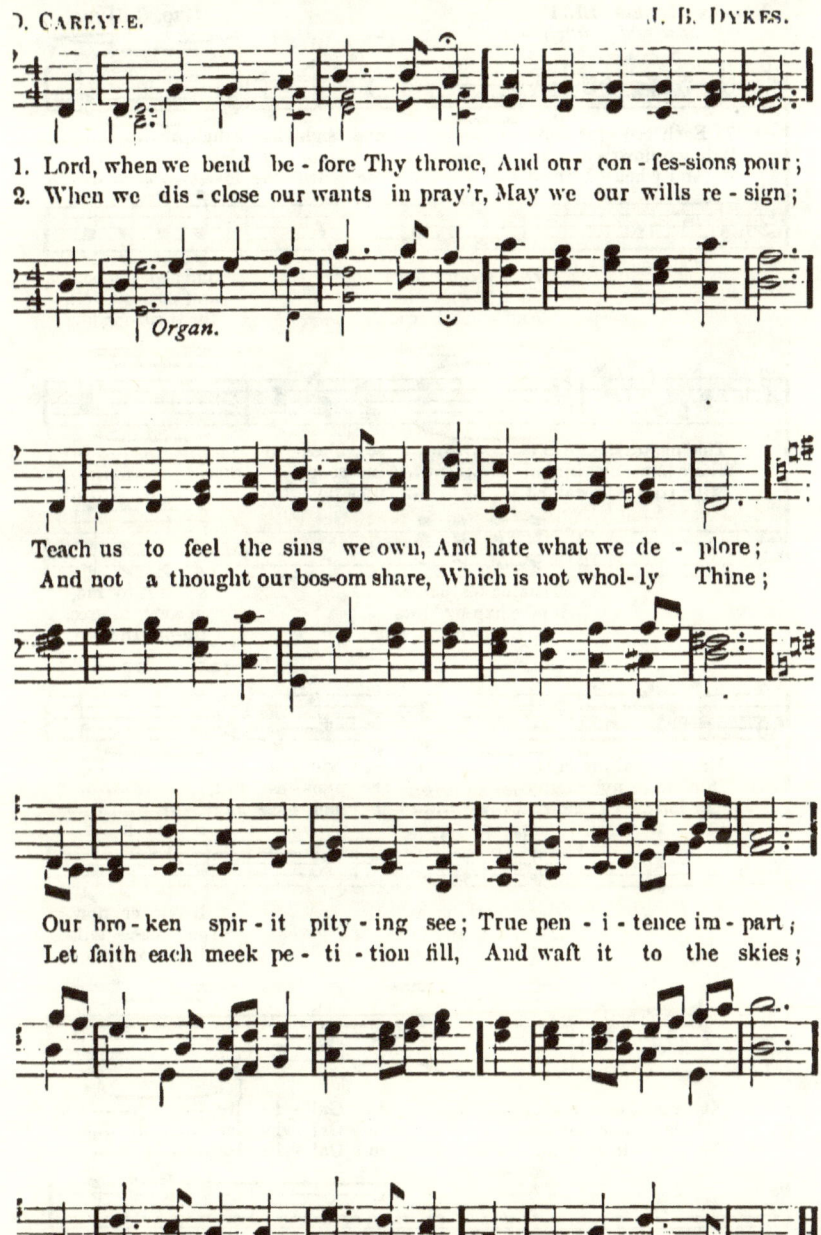

1. Lord, when we bend be-fore Thy throne, And our con-fes-sions pour;
2. When we dis-close our wants in pray'r, May we our wills re-sign;

Teach us to feel the sins we own, And hate what we de - plore;
And not a thought our bos-om share, Which is not whol-ly Thine;

Our bro-ken spir-it pity-ing see; True pen-i-tence im-part;
Let faith each meek pe-ti-tion fill, And waft it to the skies;

Then let a kind-ling glance from Thee Bear hope on ev-'ry heart.
And teach our hearts 'tis good-ness still, That grants it, or de-nies.

STRETCH FORTH THY HAND.

Geo. C. Hugg.
Slowly, and with great expression.
Geo. C. Hugg.

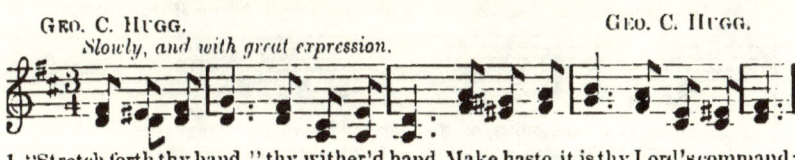

1. "Stretch forth thy hand," thy wither'd hand, Make haste, it is thy Lord's command;
2. "Stretch forth thy hand," thy sin-ful hand, Be cleansed, and join the sinless band;
3. "Stretch forth thy hand," thy giv-ing hand, Ex-pend thy gold in heathen land,
4. "Stretch forth thy hand," poor dy-ing hand; Stretch forth, it is thy Lord's command;

No palsied limb can e'er withstand Those mighty words, Stretch forth thy hand.
See, yon-der gleams the glory-land! Oh, sinner haste, "Stretch forth thy hand!"
O'er fertile plain, or Arid sand Where Christ's unknown, "Stretch forth thy hand."
Clasp firmly Christs' nail-pierced hand, 'Twill guide thee safe to Canaan's land.

CHORUS.

"Stretch forth thy hand," receive and bless, The Lord of Life and Righteousness,

HORATIUS BONAR. GEO. C. HUGG.

1. Lord, give me light to do Thy work, For on-ly, Lord, from Thee
2. The way is nar-row, of-ten dark, With lights and shadows strewn:
3. Oh, send me light to do Thy work! More light, more wis-dom give;
4. The work is Thine, not mine, O Lord; It is Thy race we run;

Can come the light, by which these eyes The way of life can see.
I wan-der oft, and think it Thine, When walking in my own.
Then shall I work Thy work in-deed, While on Thine earth I live.
Give light! and then shall all I do, Be well and tru-ly done.

CHORUS.

Send me light! send me light! Light a-long the toilsome way!
Send me light, send me light,

Send me light, dear Lord, that I may labor on, Till I rest in e-ter-nal day.

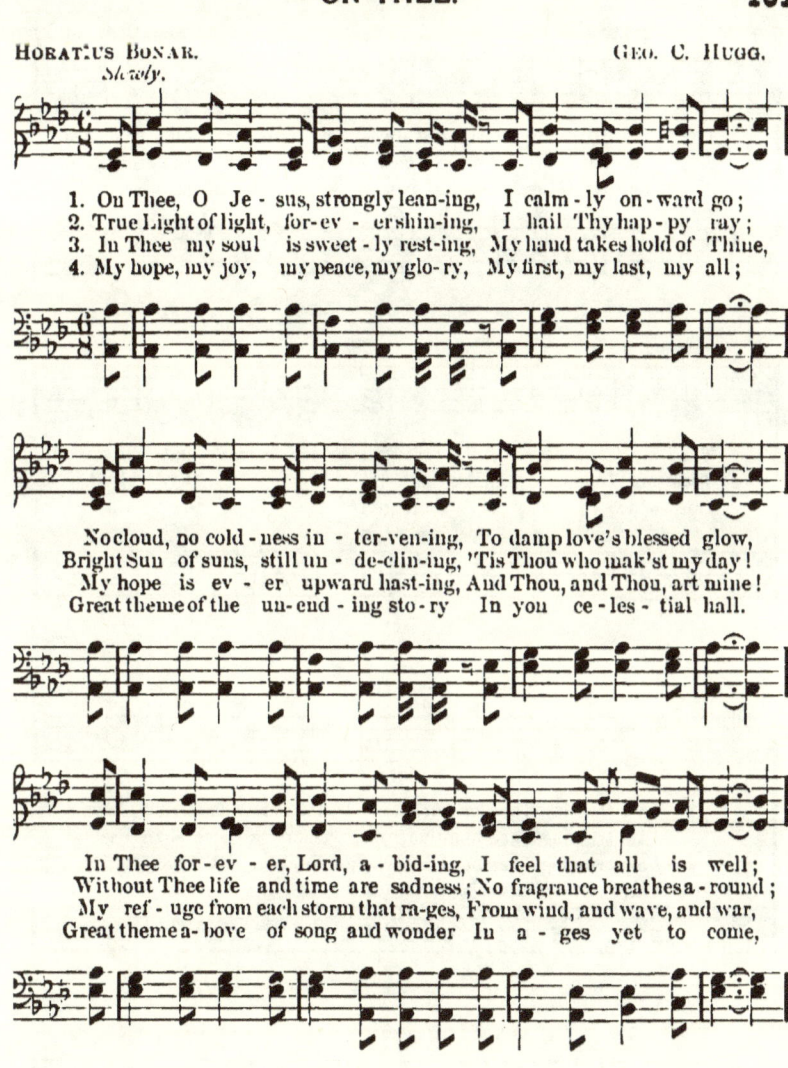

THINE.

F. R. HAVERGAL. **GEO. C. HUGG.**

1. Take my life and let it be, Con-se-cra-ted, Lord, to Thee;
2. Take my feet and let them be, Swift and beau-ti-ful for Thee;
3. Take my lips and let them be, Filled with mes-sa-ges for Thee;
4. Take my mo-ments and my days, Let them flow in end-less praise;
5. Take my will and make it Thine; It shall be no long-er mine;
6. Take my love, my Lord, I pour At Thy feet its treas-ure store!

Take my hands and let them move, At the im-pulse of Thy love.
Take my voice and let me sing, Al-ways, on-ly for my King.
Take my sil-ver and my gold,—Not a mite would I with-hold.
Take my in-te-lect, and use Ev-'ry pow'r as Thou shalt choose.
Take my heart it is Thine own,—It shall be Thy roy-al Throne.
Take my-self, and I will be, Ev-er, on-ly, all for Thee.

CHORUS.

All I am, or hope to be; Con-se-crate me Lord to Thee:

Seal me with Thy blood di-vine, Make me ev-er, on-ly Thine.

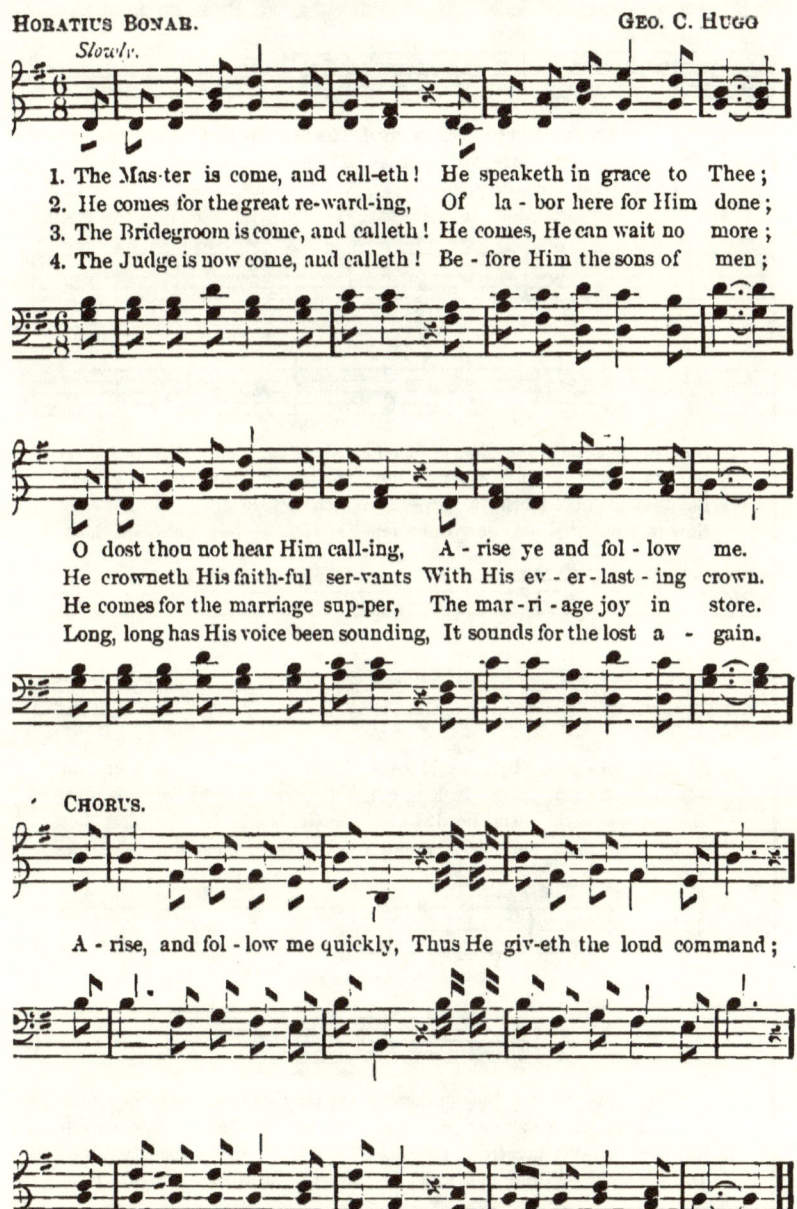

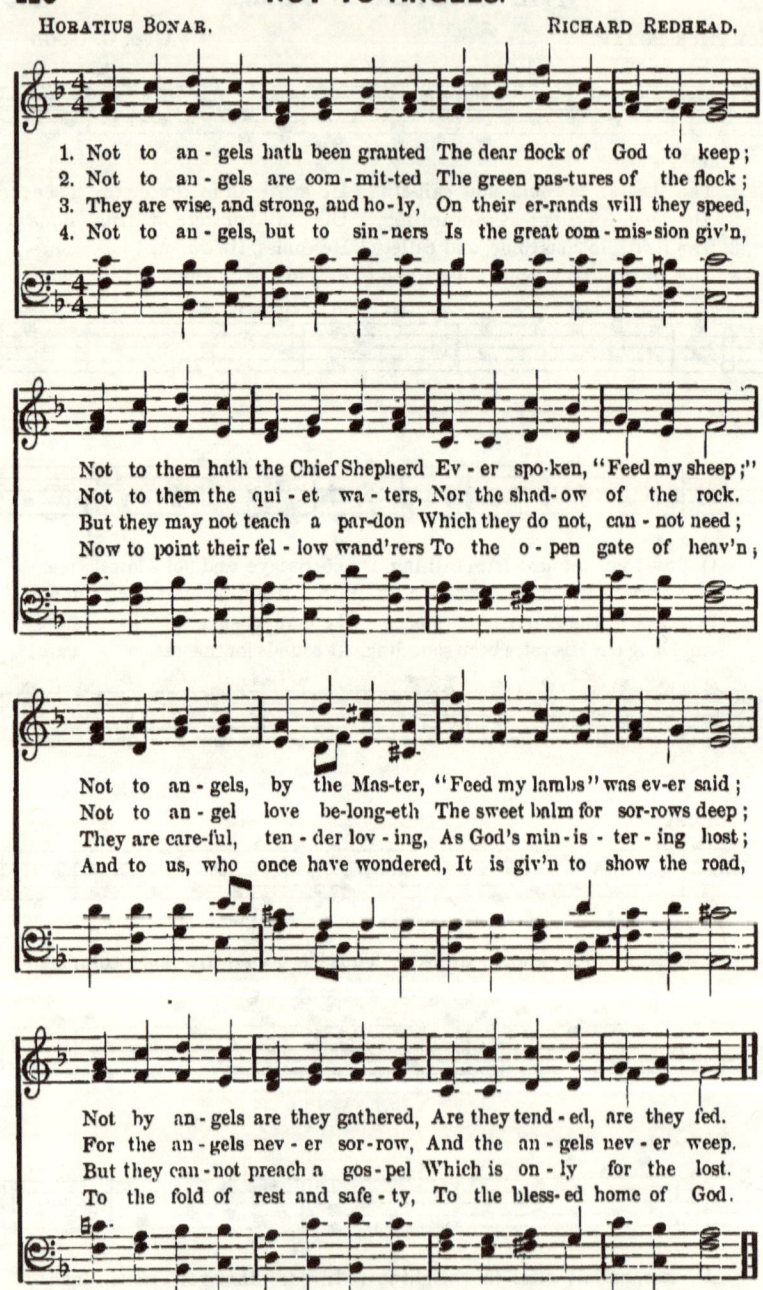

WANDERING SHEEP. 117

HORATIUS BONAR.
GEO. C. HUGG.

1. I was a wand'ring sheep, I did not love the fold,
2. The Shep-herd sought his sheep, The Fa-ther sought his child;
3. Je-sus my Shepherd is; 'Twas He that loved my soul,
4. No more a wand'ring sheep, I love to be con-trolled,

I did not love my Shepherd's voice, I would not be con-trolled:
He fol-lowed me o'er vale and hill, O'er des-erts waste and wild:
'Twas He that washed me in His blood, 'Twas He that made me whole:
I love my ten-der Shepherd's voice, I love the peace-ful fold:

I was a way-ward child, I did not love my home,
He found me nigh to death, Famished, and faint, and lone;
'Twas He that sought the lost, That found the wan-d'ring sheep,
No more a way-ward child, I seek no more to roam;

I did not love my Fa-ther's voice, I loved a-far to roam.
He bound me with the bands of love, He saved the wand'ring one.
'Twas He that brought me to the fold, 'Tis He that still doth keep.
I love my heav'nly Fa-ther's voice, I love, I love His home!

IN THE BEAUTIFUL LIGHT. Concluded.

light............ from a-bove!....How blessed to be,............... to be in the
The glorious light, How blessed, how blessed

light,............... The light of our Sav-iour's love!...............
to be in the light, the light of His love!

love!...............

SEYMOUR.

HAMMOND. VON WEBER.

1. Lord! we come be-fore Thee now, At Thy feet we humbly bow;
2. Lord, on Thee our souls de-pend, In com-pas-sion, now de-scend;
3. In Thine own ap-point-ed way, Now we seek Thee, here we stay;
4. Send some mes-sage from Thy word, That may joy and peace af-ford;

Oh! do not our suit dis-dain! Shall we seek Thee, Lord! in vain?
Fill our hearts with Thy rich grace, Tune our lips to sing Thy praise.
Lord! we know not how to go, Till a bless-ing Thou be-stow.
Let Thy Spir-it now im-part Full sal-va-tion to each heart.

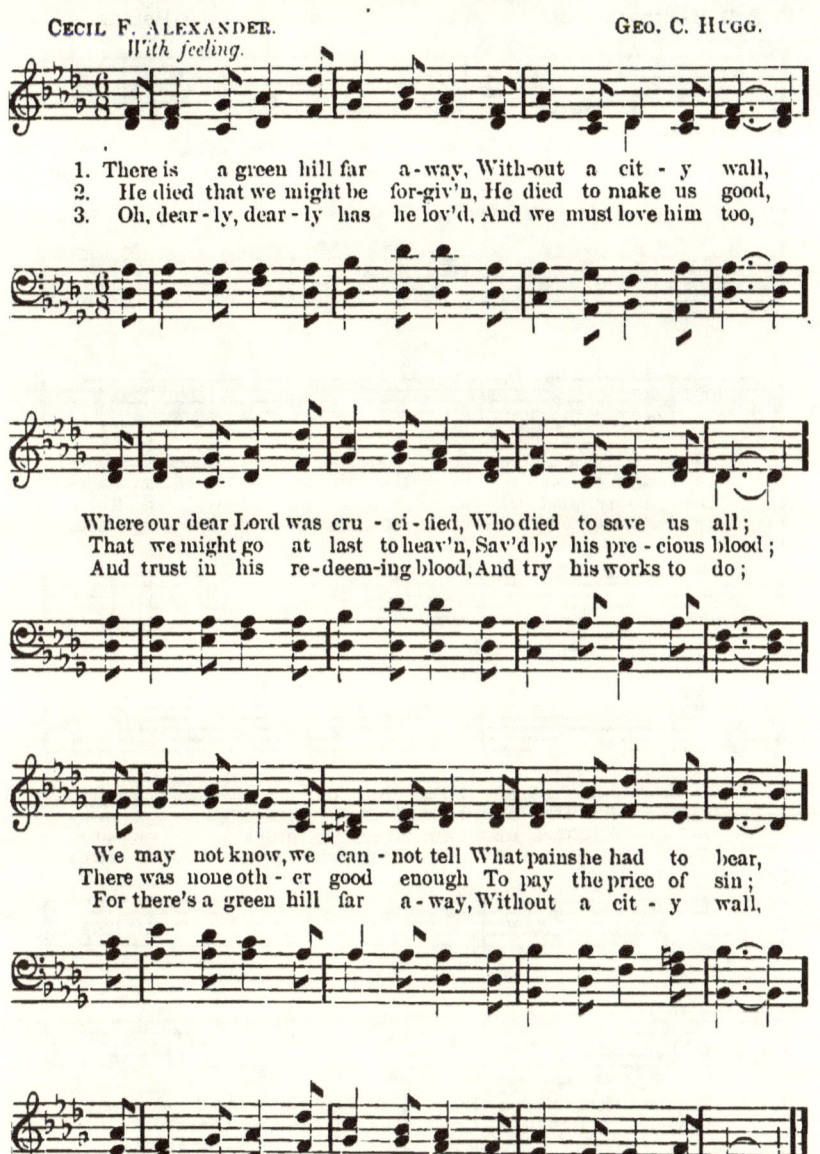

PRECIOUS SAVIOUR. Concluded. 127

CHORUS.

O Saviour, precious Saviour, Whom yet unseen we love,
O name of might and favor, All other names above.

IT IS NOT DYING.

C. MALAN.   M. MOSES.

1. No, no, it is not dying To go unto our God; This gloomy earth for-
2. No, no, it is not dying Heav'n's citizen to be; A crown immortal
3. No, no, it is not dying To hear this gracious word, Receive a Father's
4. No, no, it is not dying The shepherd's voice to know, His sheep He ever
5. No, no, it is not dying To wear a lordly crown; Among God's people
6. Oh, no, it is not dying, Thou Saviour of mankind: There streams of love are

saking, Our journey homeward taking A-long the starry road.
wearing, And rest unbroken sharing. From care and conflict free.
blessing, For evermore possessing The favor of the Lord.
leadeth, His peaceful flock He feedeth, Where living pastures grow.
dwelling, The glorious triumph swelling Of Him whose sway we own.
flowing, No hindrance ever knowing; Here drops alone we find.

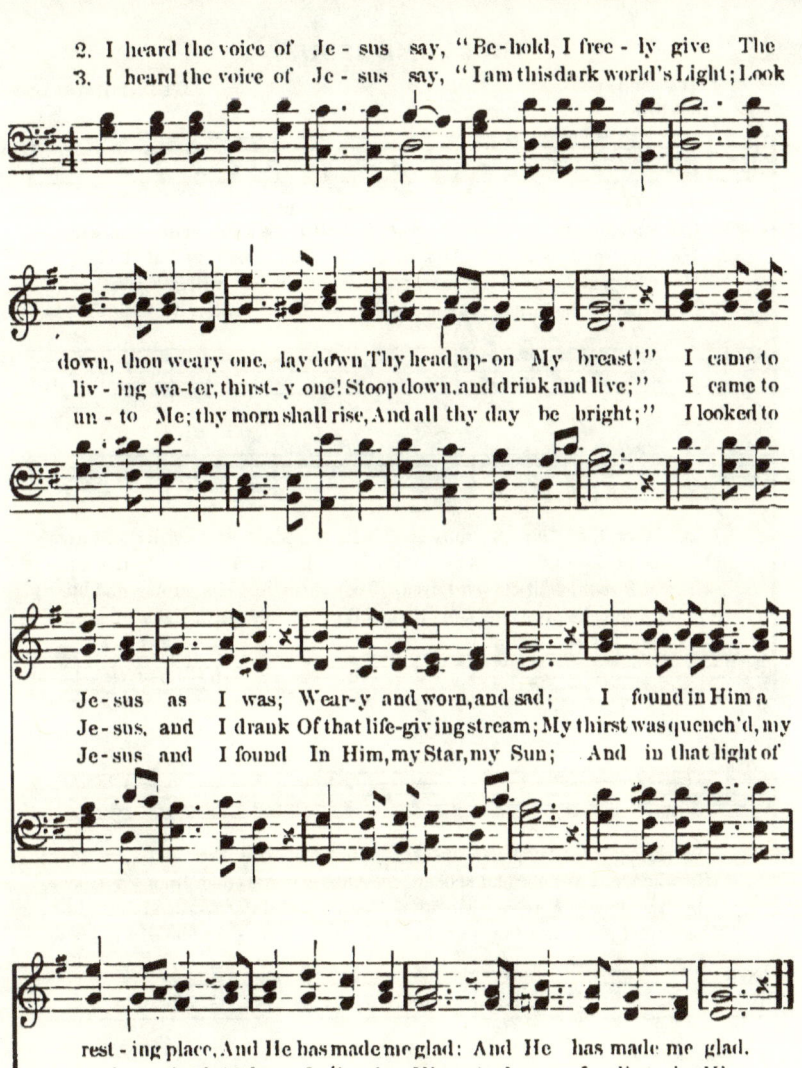

132. THIS SAME JESUS.

F. R. HAVERGAL. *Earnestly.*
GEO. C. HUGG.

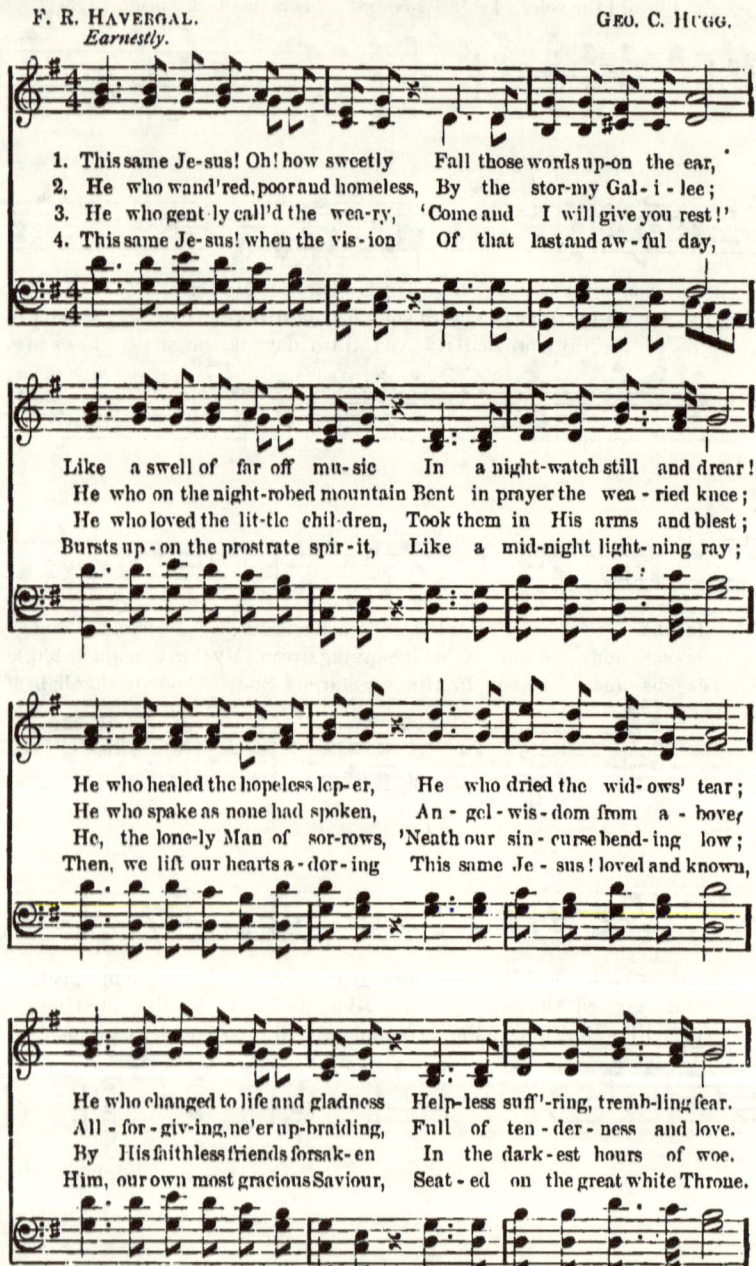

1. This same Je-sus! Oh! how sweetly   Fall those words up-on the ear,
2. He who wand'red, poor and homeless,   By the stor-my Gal-i-lee;
3. He who gent-ly call'd the wea-ry,   'Come and I will give you rest!'
4. This same Je-sus! when the vis-ion   Of that last and aw-ful day,

Like a swell of far off mu-sic   In a night-watch still and drear!
He who on the night-robed mountain   Bent in prayer the wea-ried knee;
He who loved the lit-tle chil-dren,   Took them in His arms and blest;
Bursts up-on the prostrate spir-it,   Like a mid-night light-ning ray;

He who healed the hopeless lep-er,   He who dried the wid-ows' tear;
He who spake as none had spoken,   An-gel-wis-dom from a-bove;
He, the lone-ly Man of sor-rows,   'Neath our sin-curse bend-ing low;
Then, we lift our hearts a-dor-ing   This same Je-sus! loved and known,

He who changed to life and gladness   Help-less suff'-ring, trem-bling fear.
All-for-giv-ing, ne'er up-braiding,   Full of ten-der-ness and love.
By His faithless friends forsak-en   In the dark-est hours of woe.
Him, our own most gracious Saviour,   Seat-ed on the great white Throne.

THIS SAME JESUS. Concluded.

Chorus.

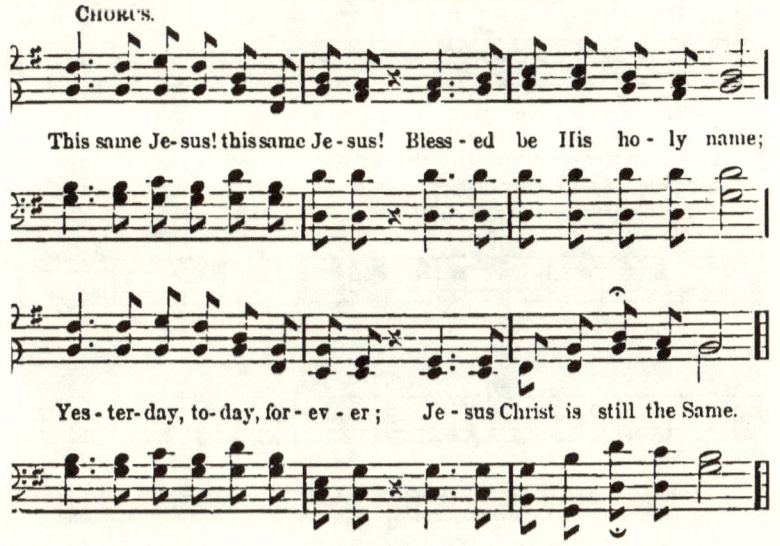

This same Je-sus! this same Je-sus! Bless-ed be His ho-ly name;
Yes-ter-day, to-day, for-ev-er; Je-sus Christ is still the Same.

BONAR.

Horatius Bonar, Geo. C. Hugg.

1. Je-ho-vah is my light and hope, Whom there-fore fear shall I?
2. Let hosts a-gainst me pitch their camp, My heart no fear shall feel,
3. One thing I of Je-ho-vah sought, For this still do I pray,
4. My help in days past Thou hast been; Do not for-sake me now;
5. Oh wait up-on Je-ho-vah, wait, Be firm and strong, he will

Je-ho-vah is my strength and life Who shall me ter-ri-fy?
Let war a-gainst me rise, in this My trust a-bid-eth still.
That in Je-ho-vah's house a-bide For-ev-er-more I may.
Nor leave me, O my God, the God Of my sal-va-tion Thou.
Strength-en the faint-ness of thy heart, Wait on Je-ho-vah still.

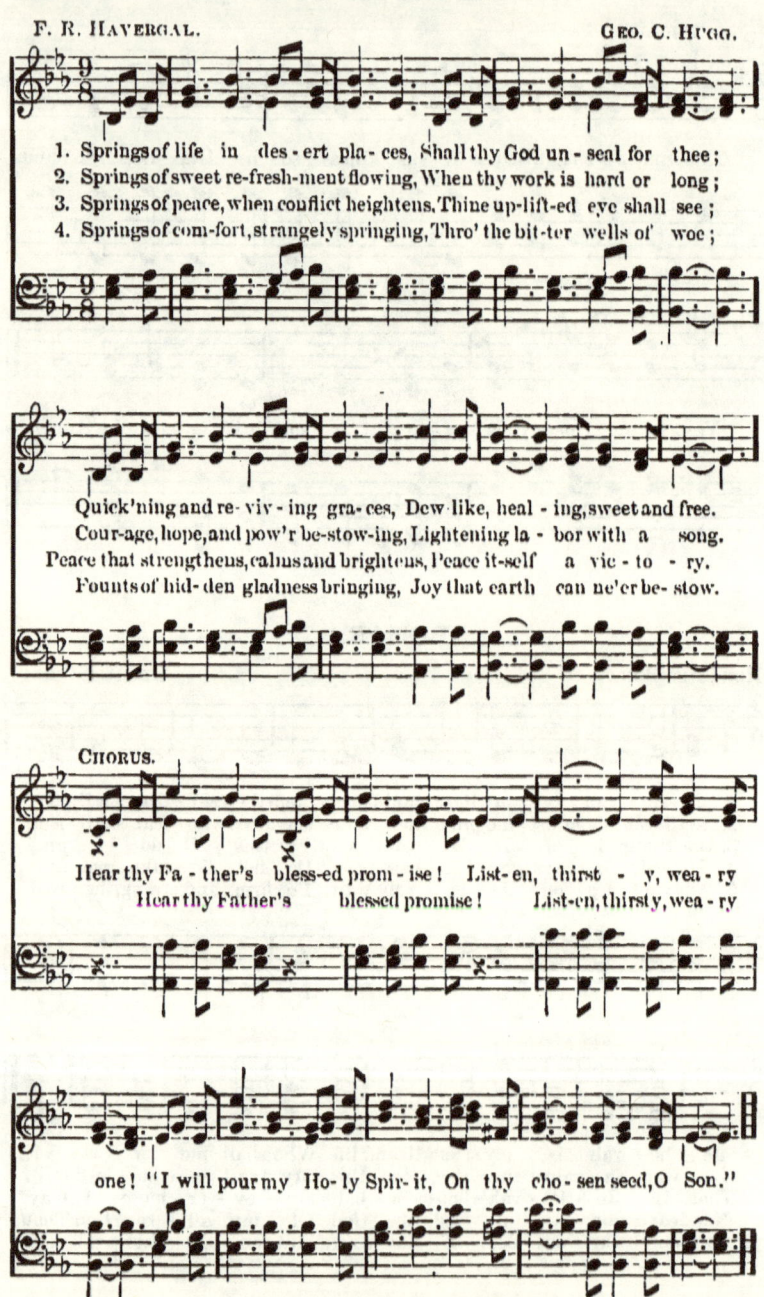

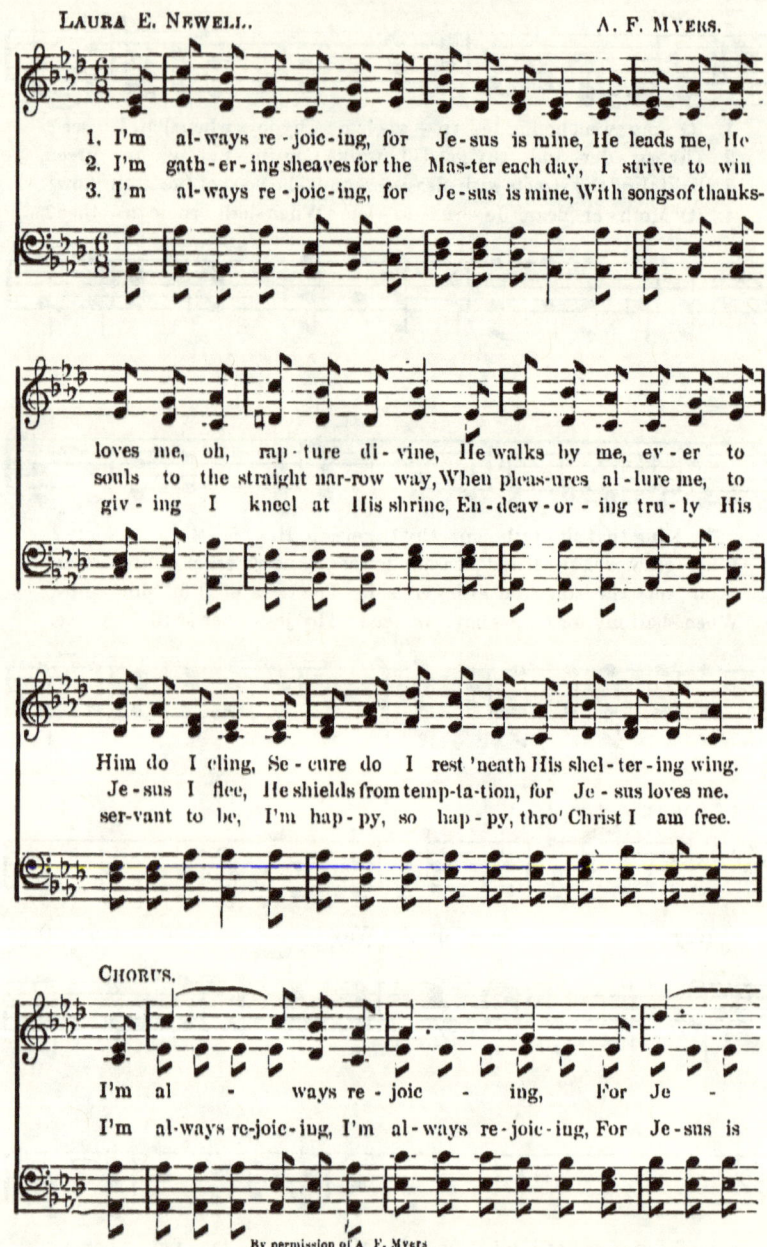

I'M ALWAYS REJOICING. Concluded. 139

HE LEADETH ME.

H. S. LOWING.

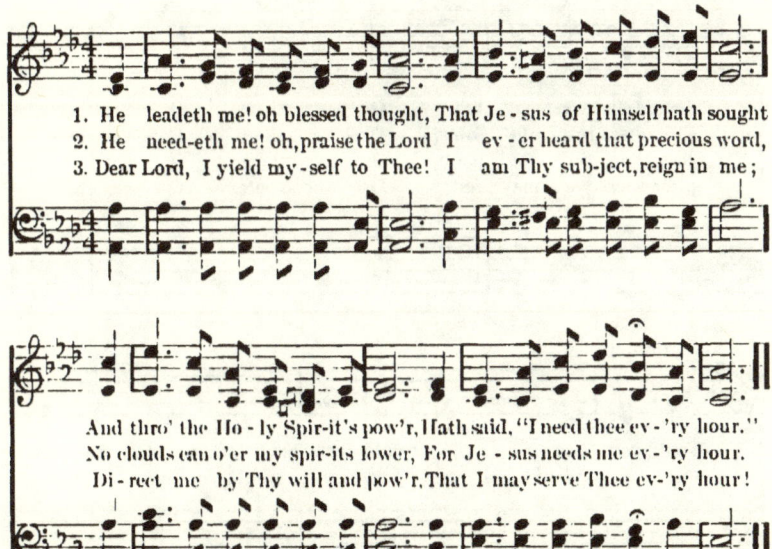

SWEET, HAPPY HOME. Concluded.

sweet,............ hap - py home? Come, then bro-ther, where the
To that sweet, hap-py home?

liv-ing wa-ters flow, Come, O come, Come, O come!
come, then brother, come.

OUR SINS ON CHRIST.

J. FAWCETT. WILLIAMS.

1. Our sins on Christ were laid; He bore the might-y load;
2. To save a world He dies; Sin-ners, be-hold the Lamb!
3. Par-don and peace a-bound; He will your sins for-give;

Our ran-som-price He ful-ly paid In groans, and tears, and blood.
To Him lift up your long-ing eyes; Seek mer-cy in His name.
Sal-va-tion in His name is found—He bids the sin-ner live.

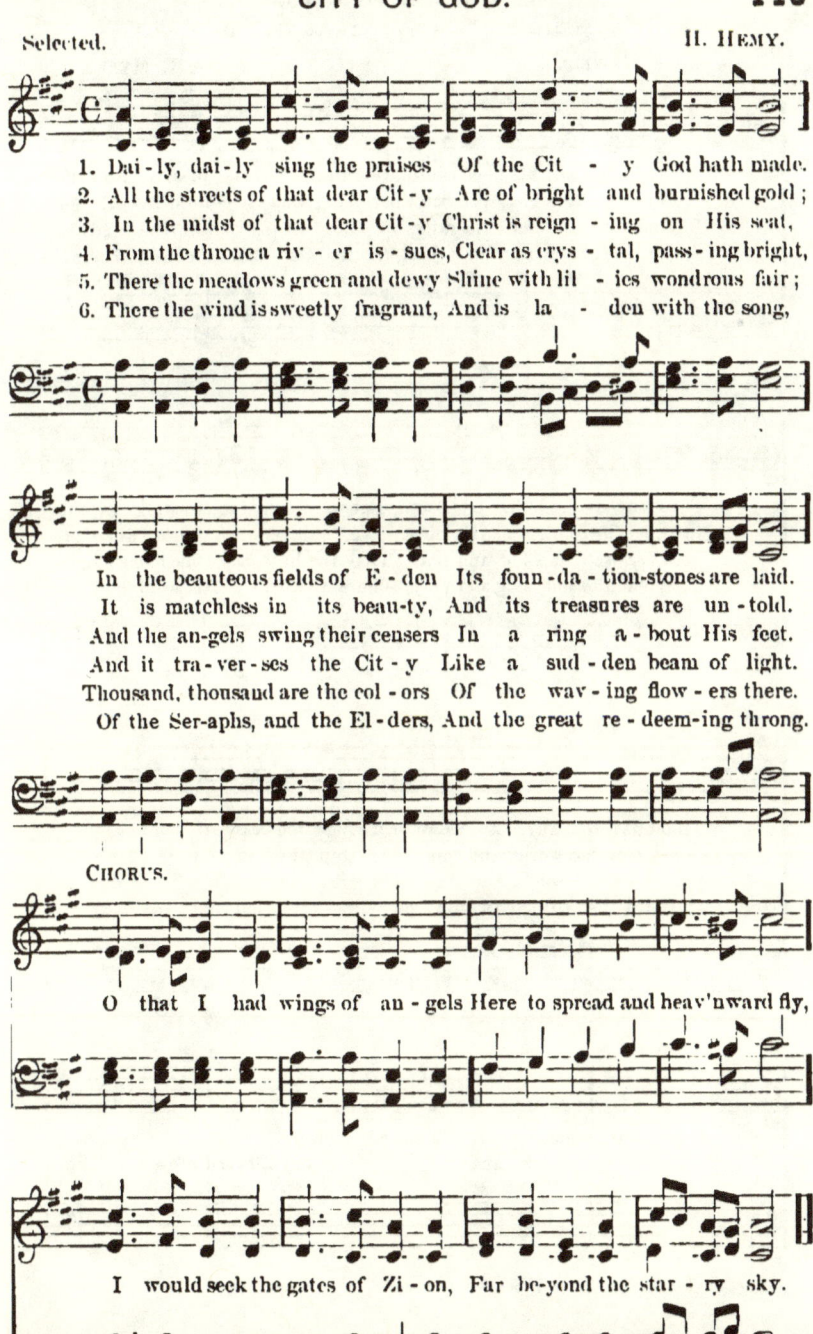

LOOK UP, LIFT UP. Concluded. 145

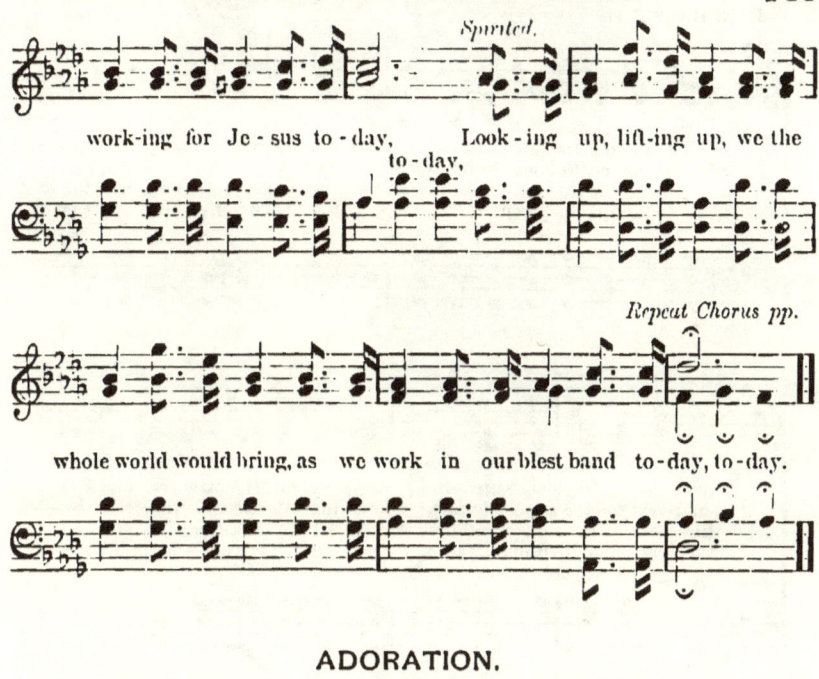

ADORATION.

JOHN BOWRING.　　　　　　　　　　　　　GEO. C. HUGG.

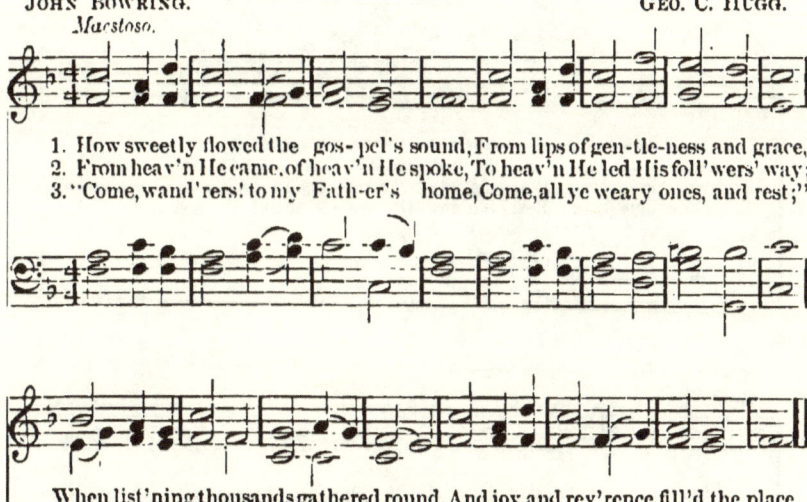

1. How sweetly flowed the gos-pel's sound, From lips of gen-tle-ness and grace,
2. From heav'n He came, of heav'n He spoke, To heav'n He led His foll'wers' way;
3. "Come, wand'rers! to my Fath-er's home, Come, all ye weary ones, and rest;"

When list'ning thousands gathered round, And joy and rev'rence fill'd the place.
Dark clouds of gloomy night He broke, Un-veiling an im - mor-tal day.
Yes, sacred Teacher; we will come, O-bey Thee, love Thee, and be blest.

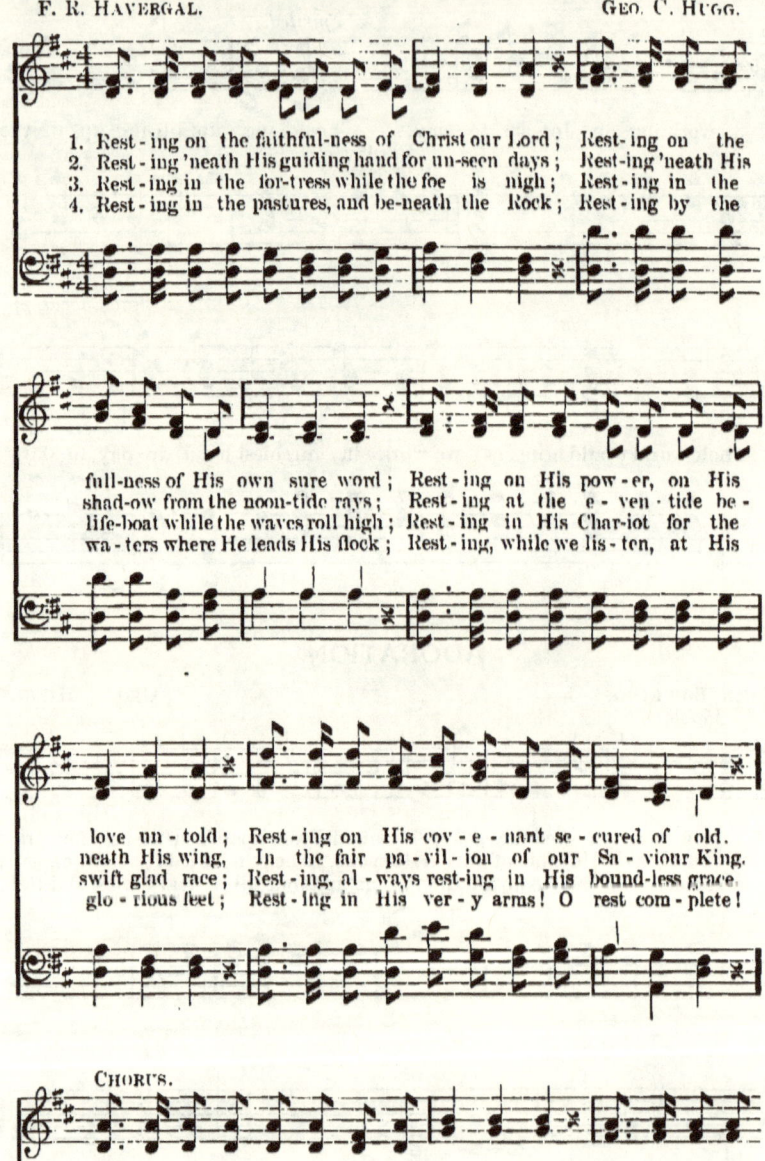

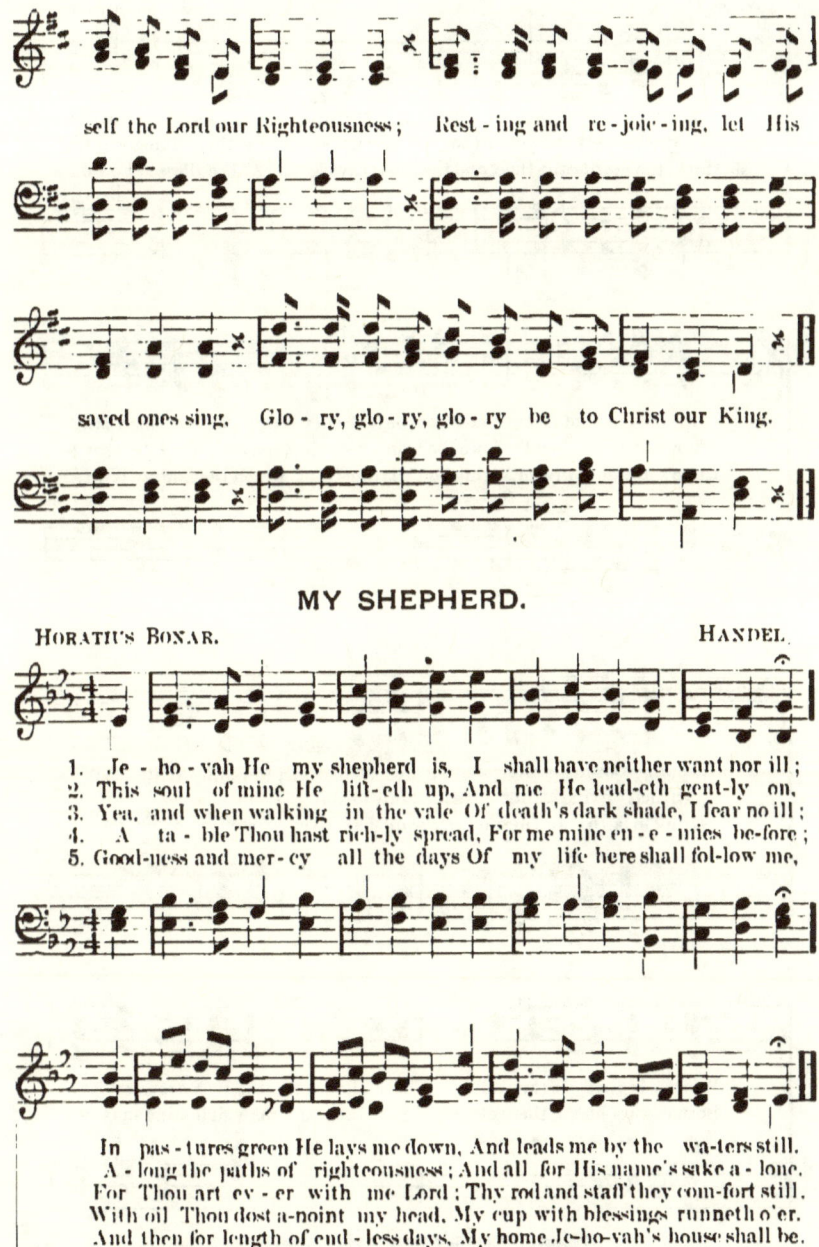

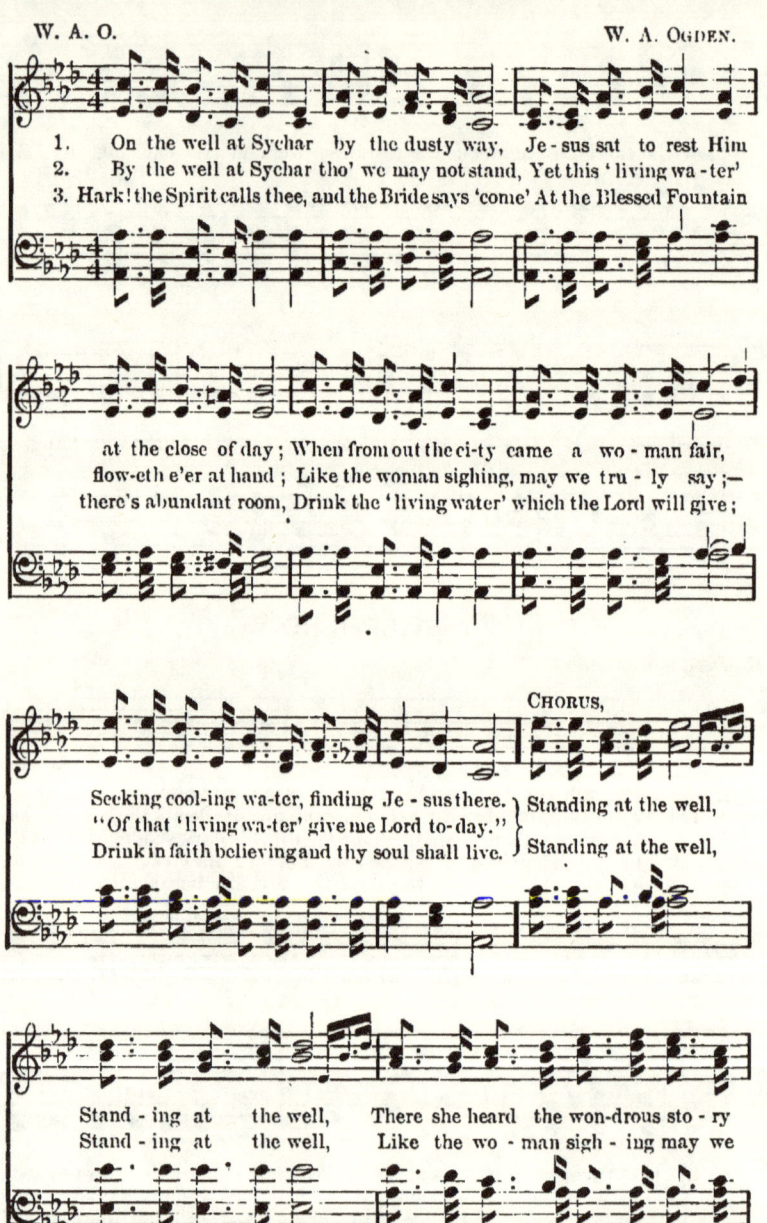

STANDING AT THE WELL. Concluded. 149

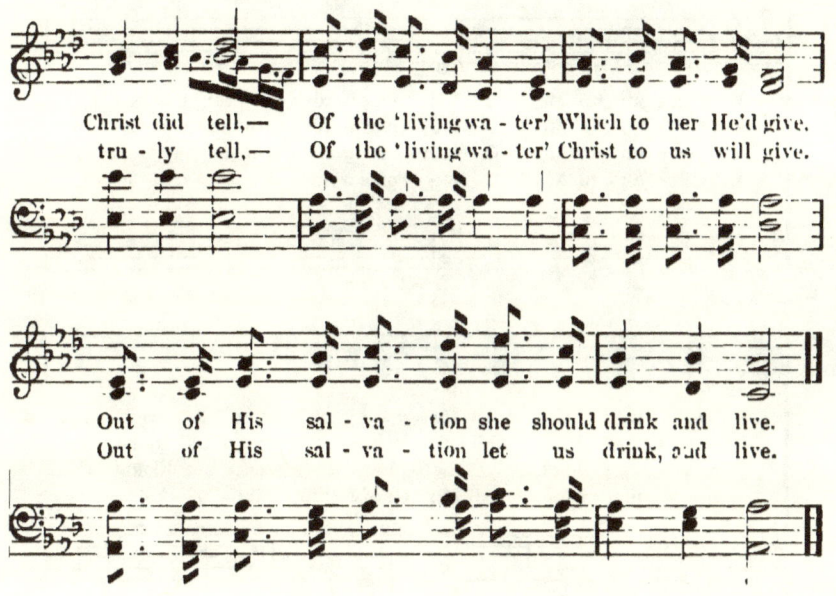

Christ did tell,— Of the 'living wa-ter' Which to her He'd give.
tru-ly tell,— Of the 'living wa-ter' Christ to us will give.

Out of His sal-va-tion she should drink and live.
Out of His sal-va-tion let us drink, and live.

SWEET IS THE WORK.

ISAAC WATTS.   LOWELL MASON.

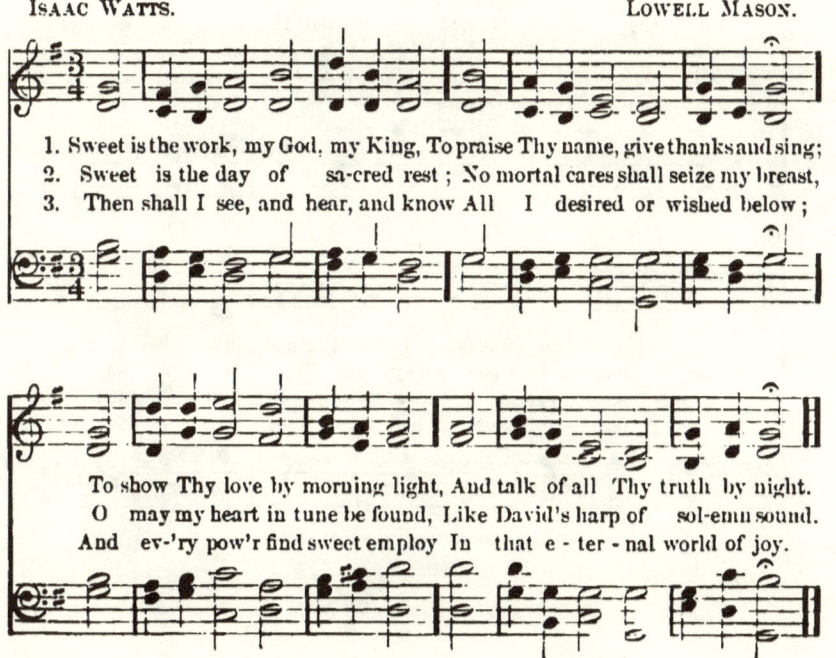

1. Sweet is the work, my God, my King, To praise Thy name, give thanks and sing;
2. Sweet is the day of sa-cred rest; No mortal cares shall seize my breast,
3. Then shall I see, and hear, and know All I desired or wished below;

To show Thy love by morning light, And talk of all Thy truth by night.
O may my heart in tune be found, Like David's harp of sol-emn sound.
And ev-'ry pow'r find sweet employ In that e-ter-nal world of joy.

1. Lo! the har-vest field is bend-ing, Who will reap the gold-en grain,
2. See the ma-ny that are wait-ing, 'Round a-bout the gold-en field,
3. Has-ten, broth-er, to the har-vest, To the har-vest of the Lord!

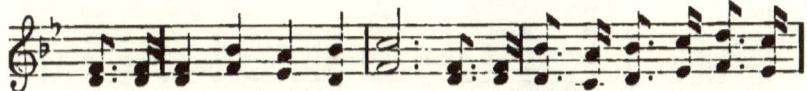

Who will bear the sheaves a - way? There are ma - ny i - dly standing
All in i - dle - ness to - day; They have themes, they have suggestions,
Gath - er sheaves from near and far, So that when the Mas - ter call-eth,

In the mark - et, and the lane, But the reap - ers, where are they?
For the la - bor and the yield, But the reap - ers, where are they?
This shall be the welcome word; "Blessed reap - ers, here they are!"

CHORUS.

Who will gather, who will gath-er? Who will gather in the gold-en grain?

Copyright in "Scriptural Songs," used by permission.

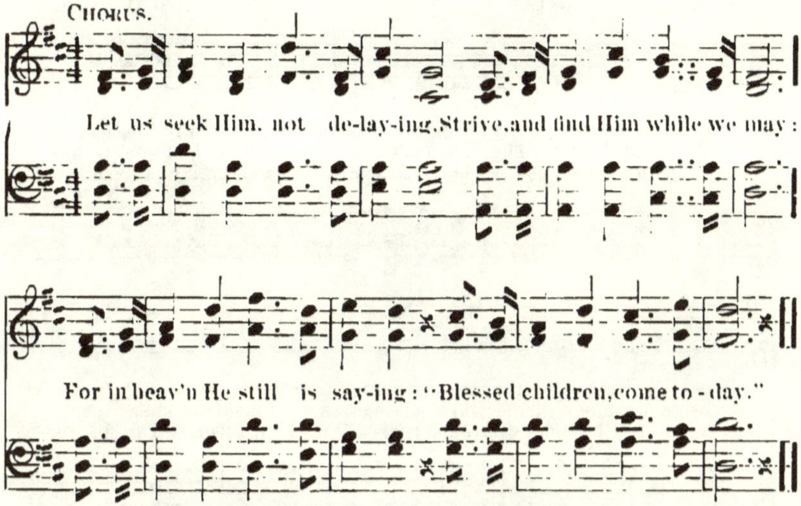

CHILDREN, COME.—Concluded.

CHORUS.

Let us seek Him, not de-lay-ing, Strive, and find Him while we may:

For in heav'n He still is say-ing: "Blessed children, come to-day."

THE HEALER.

JAMES MONTGOMERY.   Arr. by GEO. C. HUGG.

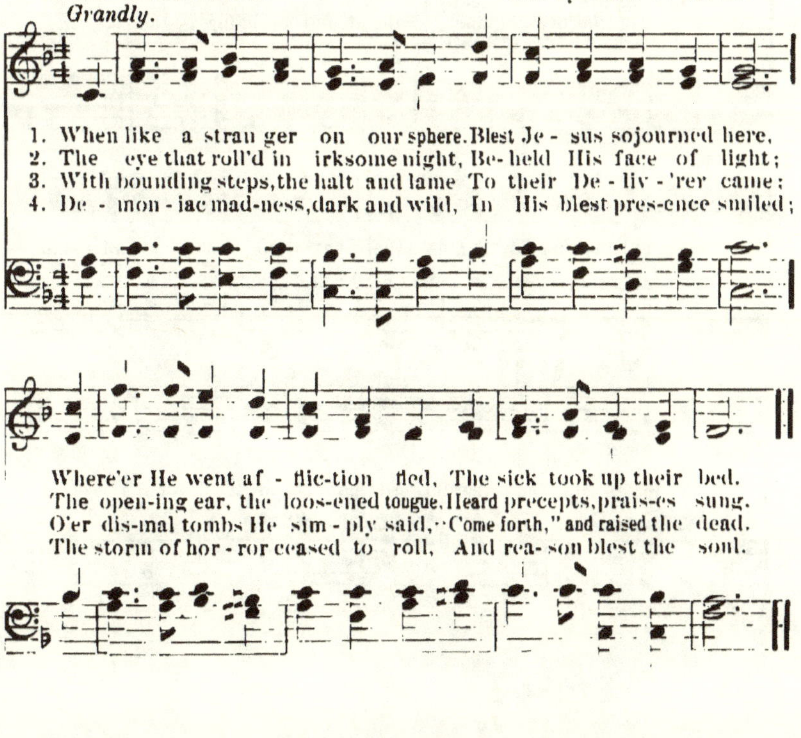

Grandly.

1. When like a stran-ger on our sphere, Blest Je-sus sojourned here,
2. The eye that roll'd in irksome night, Be-held His face of light;
3. With bounding steps, the halt and lame To their De-liv-'rer came;
4. De-mon-i-ac mad-ness, dark and wild, In His blest pres-ence smiled;

Where'er He went af-flic-tion fled, The sick took up their bed.
The open-ing ear, the loos-ened tongue, Heard precepts, prais-es sung.
O'er dis-mal tombs He sim-ply said, "Come forth," and raised the dead.
The storm of hor-ror ceased to roll, And rea-son blest the soul.

MAKE ROOM.

Geo. C. Hugg.   Geo. C. Hugg.

1. Make room for the Blessed Phy-si-cian, Who healeth the pal-sied and lame, Who cast-eth out spir-its, and dev-ils, And rais-eth the dead from the grave.
2. Make room for the Blessed Phy-si-cian, Who healeth the sick and the blind, Re-liev-ing dis-tress-es and sor-row, With pow-er, and heal-ing di-vine.
3. He com-fort-eth, healeth, and cheereth, He bringeth sal-va-tion this day, Come in-to our hearts, blessed Je-sus, Yea come, and a-bide Thou al-way.

CHORUS.

He com-eth! He com-eth! Sal-va-tion pro-

I WAS GLAD.

ANTHEM.—(Written expressly for this work.)

ADAM GEIBEL.

DOWN THE VALLEY ALONE. Continued. 167

bear me a-way, His voice I shall hear in ten-der-est tone;
praise on my lips, The way, tho' to me, is whol-ly unknown;

I shall tremble not, nor fal-ter, but sing as I go Down the
Still I'm trusting in my Sav-iour, and fear not to go Down the

CHORUS.

val-ley of the shadow all a-lone. Down the val-ley............ of the
val-ley of the shadow all a-lone.
                                              Down the valley

DOWN THE VALLEY ALONE. Concluded.

ST. PETER.

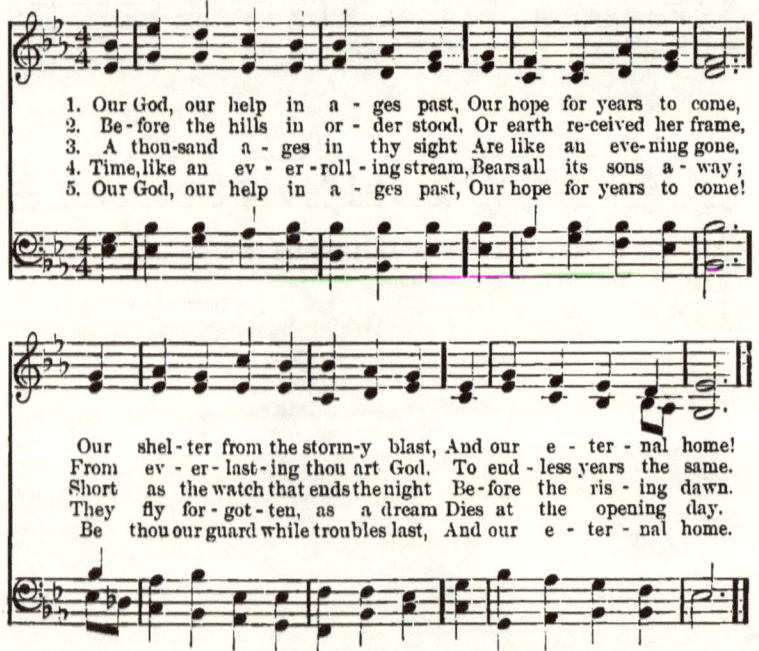

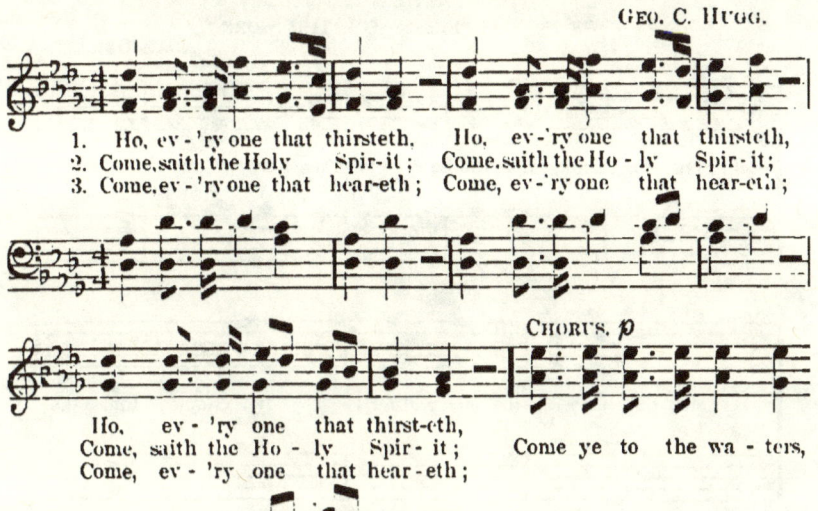

PRAISE THE LORD, O MY SOUL. Continued. 171

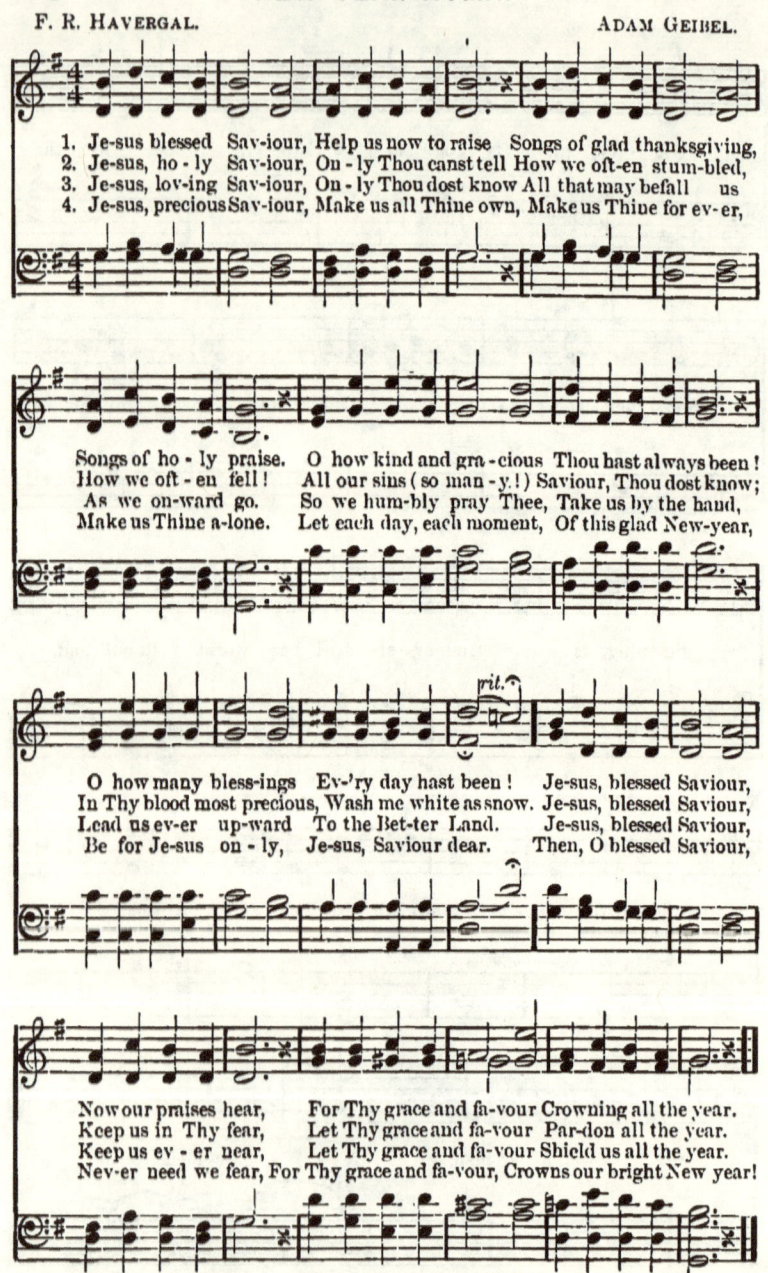

ONWARD. Concluded.

bids us forward go, Marching on-ward like a mighty arm-y,
Sa-tan's hosts are fly-ing ev-'ry-where!...... Then for-ward! on-ward!
Christ our ris-en Cap-tain, Leads a-gain His Mighty for-ces far and near.

SONG OF TRIUMPH.
Geo. C. Hugg.

1. Al-le-lu-ia! Sing to Je-sus! His the scep-tre, His the throne;
2. Hark! the songs of Ho-ly Zi-on Thunder like a might-y flood:
3. Al-le-lu-ia! Bread of heav-en, Thou on earth our food our stay;
4. Glo-ry be to God the Fa-ther! Glo-ry be to Christ the Son!

Al-le-lu-ia! His the triumph, His the vic-to-ry a-lone.
"Je-sus out of ev-'ry nation, Hath redeemed us by His blood."
Al-le-lu-ia! Here the sin-ful, Flee to Thee from day to day.
Glo-ry to the Ho-ly Spir-it! One in three, and three in One. A-men.

PRAISE YE.

181

Recessional.

Geo. C. Hugg.   Geo. C. Hugg.

182   PRAISE YE. Continued.

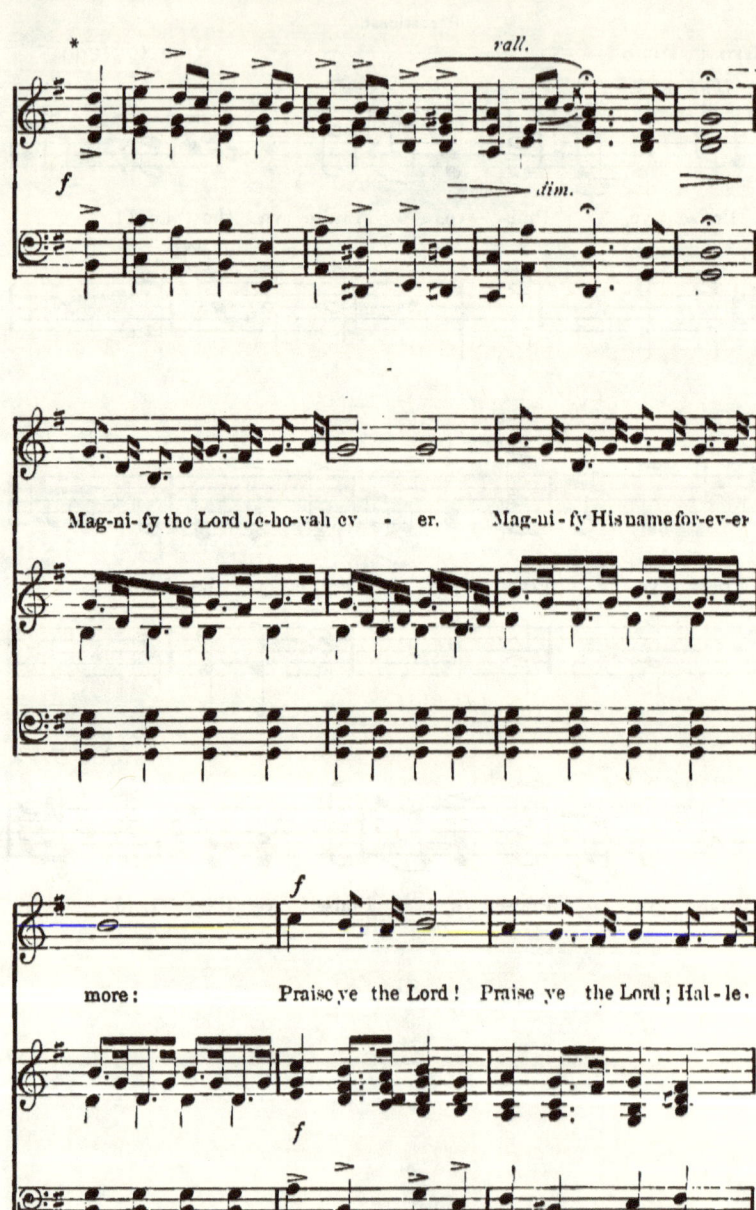

* Barri.

184 VICTORY!
Processional.

Arr. by Geo. C. Hugg. Arr. by Geo. C. Hugg.

Chorus.

We march, we march to vic-to-ry! With the cross of the Lord be-fore us, With His lov-ing Eye look-ing down from the sky, And His Ho-ly Arm spread o'er us.

1. We come in the might of the Lord of light, With meas-ured tread to meet Him; And we
2. We tread to the roll of the or-gan swell, With watchword du-ly giv-en; And we
3. Then on-ward we march our arms to prove, With Christ's own flag be-fore us; With His

VICTORY! Concluded. 185

put to flight the ar-mies of night, That the sons of the day might greet Him.
urge the Prince of the hosts of hell, To fight for the gates of Heav - en.
Eye of love looking down from above, And His ho-ly Arm spread o'er us

CHORUS.

We march, we march to vic - to - ry! With the

cross of the Lord be - fore us, With His lov - ing Eye look-ing

186. MY ROCK AND FORTRESS.

Psalm XXXI. Arr. Berthold Tours.

2. Fear not, for be-hold I bring you Tidings glad of Je-sus' birth,
3. Eag-er-ly, the Shepherds hastened, O'er the dew-beads clear, and bright;

Shepherds o'er their flocks were watching, As their fa-thers did of old.
Un-to God, a-lone be glo-ry, And to man be peace on earth.
With a star-ry guide be-fore them, Whilst around them all was light.

Sud-den-ly a mighty an-gel, Came from heav'n in raiment bright;
Haste thee now to Bethlehem's manger, There thou'lt find the New-born Child;
Soon they stood at Bethlehem's manger, Viewing there God's on-ly Son;

And the watching, wond'ring Shepherds, Trembled sore, with dire af-fright.
Christ the Lord by Prophets spoken, Ho-ly, spot-less, un-de-filed.
While the Myr-iad hosts of Heaven, Joined the song on earth be-gun.

ON A STARRY NIGHT. Concluded.

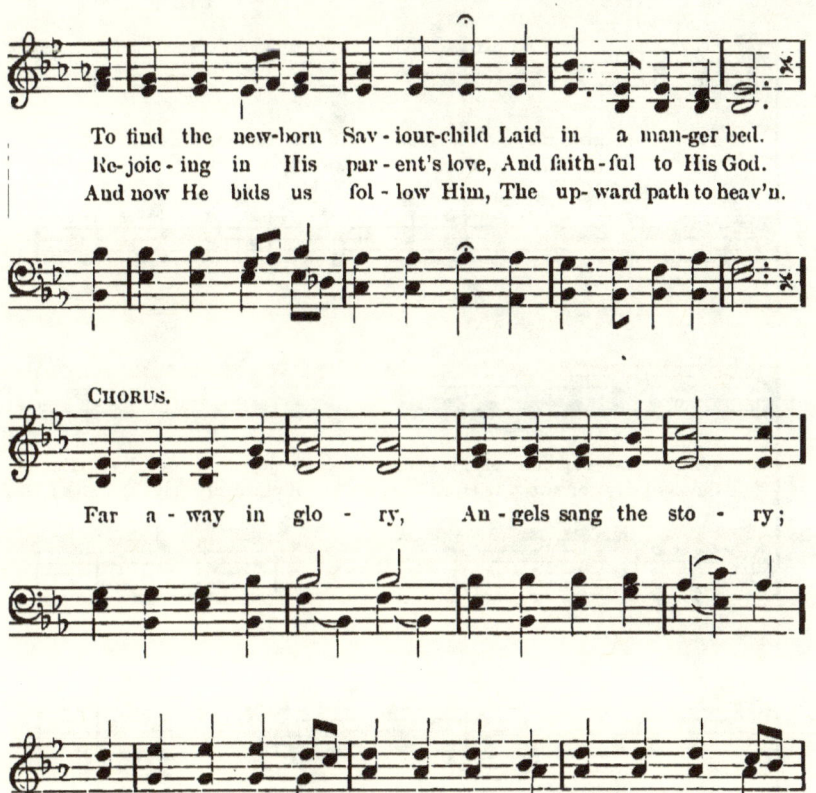

To find the new-born Sav-iour-child Laid in a man-ger bed.
Re-joic-ing in His par-ent's love, And faith-ful to His God.
And now He bids us fol-low Him, The up-ward path to heav'n.

CHORUS.

Far a-way in glo - ry, An-gels sang the sto - ry;

And we on earth may join the song Loud chant-ed by the

THE ANGELS' SONG.

196

C. H. G.
C. H. Gabriel.

1. We will sing the dear old story o'er a-gain,
How the an-gels came to shep-herds on the plain,
Prais-ing God, and say-ing: "peace, good-will to men,"
While the host of heav-en joined the glad re-frain.

2. In a man-ger, lo! the in-fant King be-hold!
Rude-ly pil-lowed, with His moth-er on the hay;
With the beasts of bur-den—low-li-ness un-told—
He has come to take the sting of death a-way.

SING, MERRILY SING. Concluded. 203

sing, mer-ri-ly sing, Let murm'rings for- ev - er cease..............
mer-ri-ly sing.

COME AND WORSHIP.

JAMES MONTGOMERY. ROB'T FINCH.

1. An - gels from the realms of glo - ry, Wing your flight o'er all the earth;
2. Shepherds in the field a - bid-ing, Watching o'er your flocks by night;
3. Sag - es leave your con - tem-plations, Brighter vis - ions beam a - far;

Ped.

Ye who sang Cre - a - tion's sto - ry, Now proclaim Mes - si - ah's birth;
God with man is now re - sid - ing, Yon - der shines the in - fant light;
Seek the great De-sire of na - tions, Ye have seen His na - tal star;

Ped.

Come and wor-ship, come and wor-ship, Worship, Christ, the new-born King.

CHRIST IS RISEN. Concluded. 207

Christ is ris - en! Christ is ris - en! He hath burst His bonds in twain;
Christ is ris - en! Christ is ris - en! He hath burst His bonds in twain;
Christ is ris - en! Christ is ris - en! He hath burst His bonds in twain;

Christ is ris - en! Christ is ris - en! Al - le - lu - ia! Swell the strain!
Christ is ris - en! Christ is ris - en! Al - le - lu - ia! Swell the strain!
Christ is ris - en! Christ is ris - en! O'er the u - ni - verse to reign.

HARK! THE SONG.

1. Hark! bright an-gels sweetly sing In the glo-rious Eas-ter sky,
2. Vain - ly soldiers tried to hold Ho - ly Je - sus in the grave,
3. For on this day, Je - sus said, He would rise in triumph high
4. We must die as Je - sus died, But we hope with Him to rise,

How from death the Lord our King, Rose henceforth no more to die.
Sealed the stone, as they were told At the entrance to the cave.
Rise all glo-rious from the dead; Clothed with light and majes-ty.
And in bod - ies glo - ri - fied Reign with Him beyond the skies

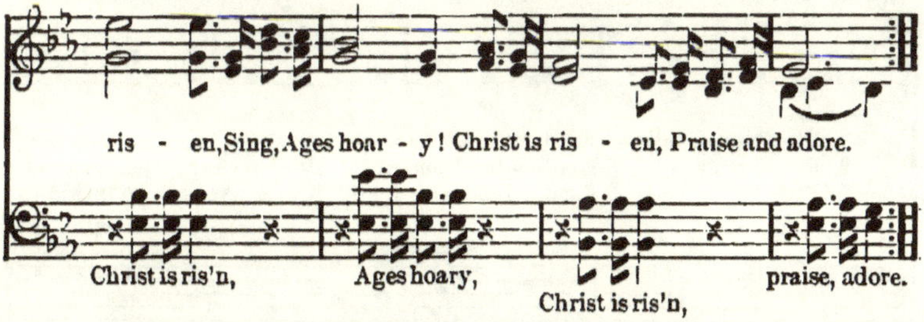

OUR CHEERFUL SONG. Concluded. 211

ris - en, Sing, Ages hoar - y! Christ is ris - en, Praise and adore.

Christ is ris'n,   Ages hoary,   Christ is ris'n,   praise, adore.

HAIL THE DAY THAT SEES HIM RISE.

1. Hail the day that sees Him rise, Hal - le - lu - jah! Glorious to His
2. There the glorious triumph waits, Hal - le - lu - jah! Lift your heads, e-
3. Still for us He in - ter-cedes, Hal - le - lu - jah! His pre-vail-ing
4. What, though parted from our sight, Hal-le - lu - jah! Far a-bove yon

na - tive skies! Hal - le - lu - jah! Christ, a-while to mor-tals giv'n,
ter - nal gates! Hal - le - lu - jah! Christ hath vanquished death and sin;
death He pleads; Hal - le - lu - jah! Near Him-self pre - pares a place,
star - ry height; Hal - le - lu - jah! Thith-er our af - fec - tions rise,

Hal - le - lu - jah! Enters now the gates of Heav'n, Hal-le - lu - jah!
Hal - le - lu - jah! Take the King of glory in, Hal - le - lu - jah!
Hal - le - lu - jah! Great Forerunner of our race, Hal - le - lu - jah!
Hal - le - lu - jah! Follow'ng Him beyond the skies, Halle - lu - jah!

BELLS OF EASTER-TIME. Concluded.

CHORUS.

Ring, ring, ring hap-py bells, Ring hap-py bells of Eas-ter-time,
Ring, ring, ring, ring,

Ring, ring, Ring hap-py bells, Ring hap-py bells of Eas-ter-time.
Ring, ring, ring, ring,

THE KING OF GLORY.

ROBERT FINCH.

1. Our Lord is ris-en from the dead; Our Jesus is gone up on high; The
2. There His triumphal char-iot waits, And angels chant the sol-emn lay; Lift
3. Loose all your bars of mas-sy light, And wide unfold the' ethereal scene; He
4. Who is the King of Glo-ry? Who? The Lord, that all our foes o'ercame; The

pow'rs of hell are cap-tive led, Dragg'd to the por-tals of the sky.
up your heads, ye heav'n-ly gates; Ye ev-er-last-ing doors, give way;'
claims these man-sions as His right; Receive the King of Glo-ry in!
world, sin, death, and hell o'er-threw; And Jesus is the Conqu'ror's name.

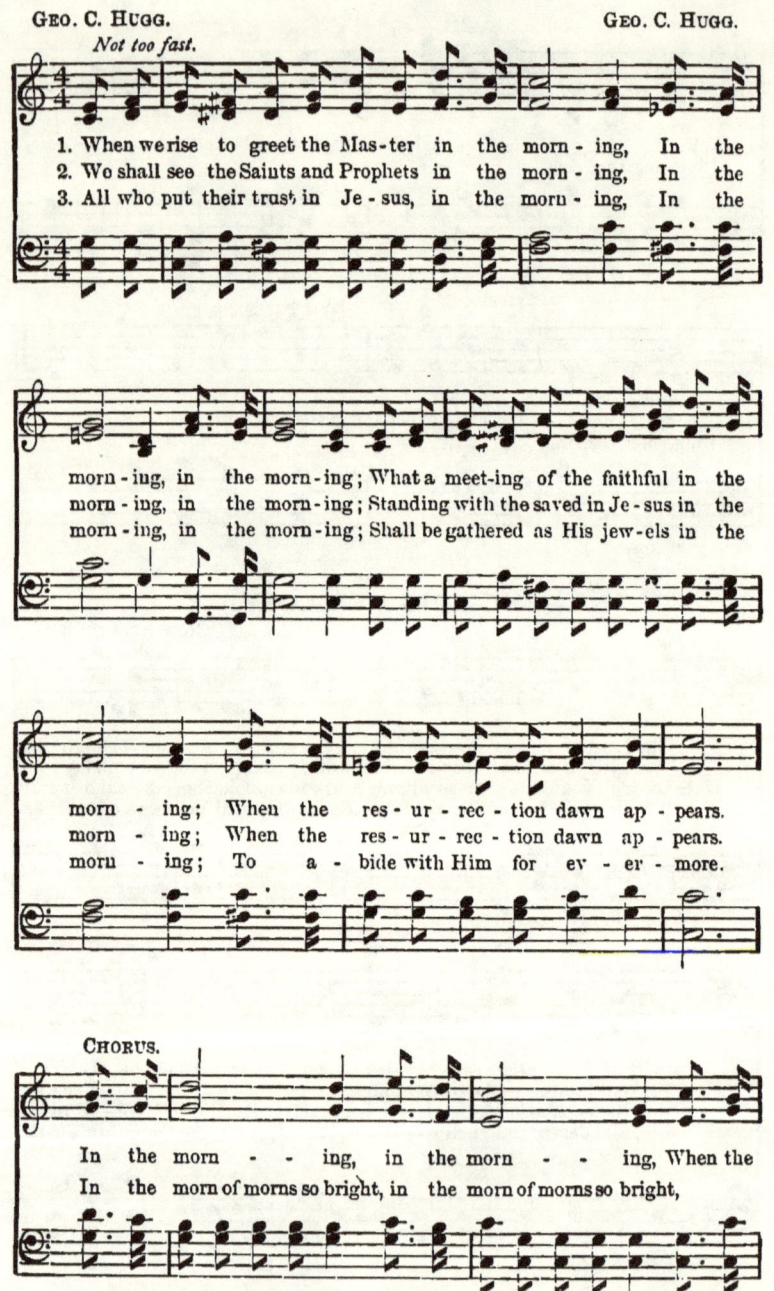

RING THE EASTER BELLS. Concluded. 217

Bells............... Ring the hap - py Eas-ter Bells...............
hap-py Eas-ter Bells, The Eas-ter Bells.

Repeat Chorus softly after last verse, ad lib.

ALLELUIA!

J. M. NEALE.   JOSEPH BARNBY.

Al - le - lu - ia, Al - le - lu - ia, Al - le - lu - ia!

1. Ye sons and daugh-ters of the Lord! The King of Glo - ry,
2. On Sun - day morn, at break of day, The faith-ful wom-en
3. Then straight-way one in white they see, Who saith, "Ye seek the
4. When Thom- as first these tid - ings heard, He doubt - ed if it
5. "Be - hold my side, O Thom-as! see, My hands, my feet, I
6. When Thom- as saw that wound - ed side, The truth no lon - ger
7. How blest are they who have not seen, And yet whose faith hath

King a-dored, This day Himself from death restored, Alle - lu - ia!
went their way, To see the place where Jesus lay, Al - le - lu - ia!
Lord; but he Is ris'n, and gone to Gal-i-lee, Al - le - lu - ia!
were the Lord, Un-til he came and spake this word, Alle - lu - ia!
show to thee; Nor faithless, but be - liev-ing be," Al - le - lu - ia!
he de-nied; "Thou art my Lord and God!" he cried, Alle - lu - ia!
con-stant been! For they e - ter-nal life shall win, Al - le - lu - ia!

JOY, JOY, JOY! Concluded. 219

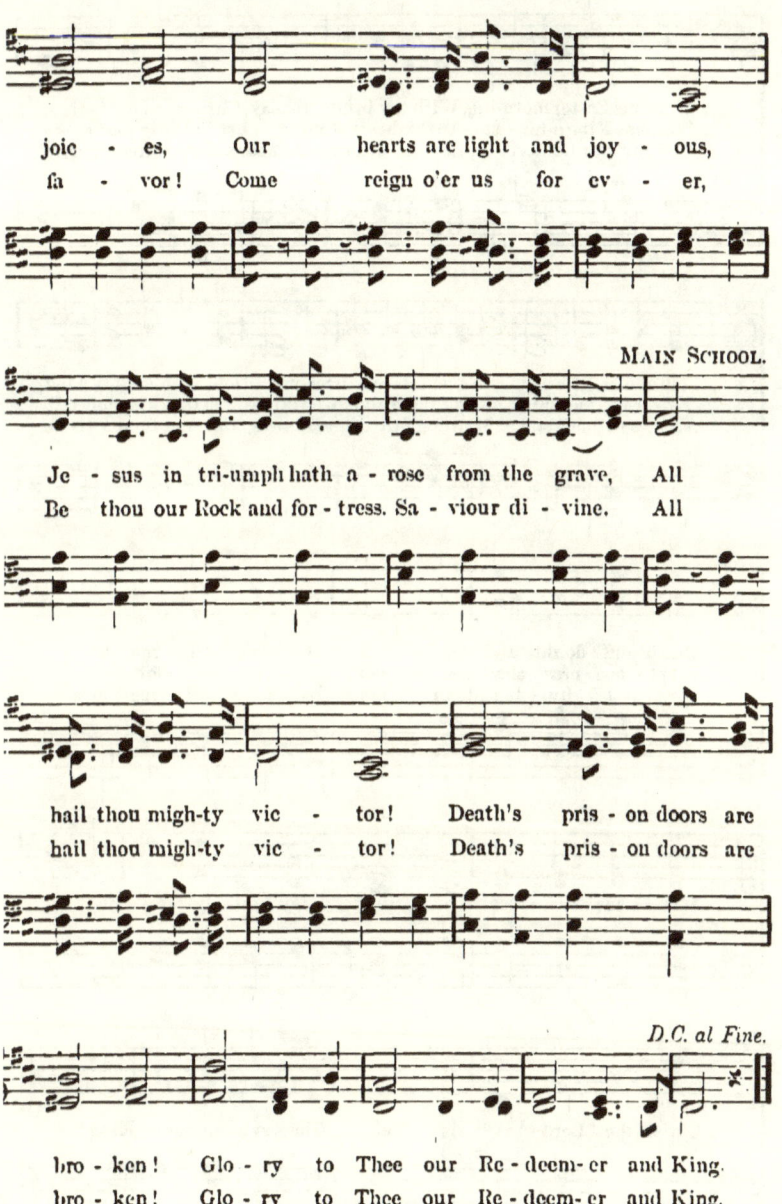

INDEX OF TITLES.

Title	PAGE
A Blessing For Me	69
A Bright World Beyond	57
Adoration	145
A Green Hill	125
A Land Without a Storm	58
All, And In All	29
Alleluia	217
All Hail the Power	47
As Oft with Worn and Weary Feet	142
Ask, Seek, Knock	110
At Anchor Riding	156
At Last	86
Bells Across the Snow	194
Bells of Easter-Time	212
Beyond	79
Bonar	133
Blessed Is He	164
Blessed Morn	190
Blest Be the Tie	39
Brightly Gleams Our Banner	70
Bring Them In	108
Callest Thou	130
Captain of Salvation	37
Carthage	55
City of God	143
Come and Worship	203
Come Home	32
Come to Me	131
Come Unto Me	150
Coming	80
Cheering Light	6
Christ Is Risen	206
Christ's Prayer in Gethsemane	48
Children, Come	154
Dost Thou See Them?	84
Down the Valley Alone	166
Dundee	31
Eastertide	208
Enter In	103
Evening	73
Even So, Amen	129
Ever Faithful	85
Everlasting Life	151
Fresh Springs	134
Galilee	94
Glad Bells	189
Glory in the Highest	188
Glory to God	198
Going Up to Zion	24
Golden Harps	76
Gospel Armor	68
Grace Abounding	50
Grateful Praise	40
Hail the Day	211
Happy In Jesus	98
Hark, My Soul	180
Hark, the Song	207
Have You Not a Word?	88
Hear the Bugle Calling	19
He Leadeth Me	139
His Promise	124
Holy Sabbath	136
Ho! Every One That Thirsteth	169
Home	63
Home, Home, Sweet Home	23
Homeward Bound	51
Hosanna	60
Humility	93
I Long to Work For Thee	43
I'm Always Rejoicing	138
In the Beautiful Light	122
In the Happy Land	25
I Shall Reach That Shore	92
Is It Nothing to Me?	106
Is Thy Cruse Almost Exhausted?	17
It Is Not Dying	127
I Was Glad	160
Jesus Knows	135
Jesus Lives	8
Jesus, Saviour, Pilot Me	53
Jesus Will Carry Me Over	118
Joy, Joy, Joy	218
Just Now	36
Just the Same	12
Land of Promise	14
Launch Out	4
Lead, Kindly Light	113
Lean On Me	107
Leave It to Him	152
Lift Me Higher	96
Light Divine	119
Light of Day	91
List, the Notes	200
Living Water	83
Looking Unto Jesus	111
Look Up, Lift Up	144
Make Room	157
Marching On with Gladness	30
More Than Conquerors	28
My Rock and Fortress	186
My Shepherd	147
My Soul Will Overcome	112
New Jerusalem	137
New Year Hymn	174
Nobody Knows But Jesus	109
No Candle nor Sun	74

Index of Titles.

Title	Page
Not a Mountain Streamlet	64
Nothing to Pay	175
Not to Angels	116
Old Hundred	59
On a Starry Night	192
On Thee	101
On to Conquest	178
Onward	176
Onward, Christian Soldiers	82
Our Cheerful Song	210
Our Sins on Christ	141
Over the Chilling Stream	158
Paradise	62
Peace on Earth	204
Perfect Peace	121
Planting a Blessing	66
Praise Him Again	11
Praise the Lord, O My Soul	170
Praise Ye	181
Praise Ye the Lord	44
Precious Saviour	126
Promptly, Sweetly, Gladly	42
Resting	146
Rich in Blessing	3
Ring the Easter Bells	216
River of Life	61
Satisfied	5
Scattering Precious Seed	72
Send Me Light	99
Seymour	123
Show Me Thy Glory	78
Singing for Jesus	56
Sing, Merrily Sing	202
Soldiers of the Cross	13
Song of Triumph	177
Songs of Love	90
Sunlight	65
Sun of My Soul	75
Standing at the Well	148
Standing There	128
Steer Toward the Light	15
St. Peter	168
Stretch Forth Thy Hand	97
Sweet, Happy Home	140
Sweet Is the Work	149
That Old, Old Story Is True	26
The Angel's Song	196
The Blessed Old Banner	38
The Bridegroom Cometh	16
The God of Love	21
The Harbor Lights of Home	22
The Healer	155
The King of Glory	213
The Master Is Come	115
The Morning	214
The Watchers	191
The Worker's Prayer	77
Toiling for Jesus	100
To Jesus Now	104
There Will Be Glory Enough	114
Thine	105
This Same Jesus	132
Trust In the Lord with All Thine Heart	33
Trusting Jesus	102
Truth Divine	87
Turning to God	159
Twine the Garland	209
Under His Shadow	120
Victory	184
Waiting at the Gates	10
Wandering Sheep	117
Wait Patiently	67
Walk In the Light	18
Welcome Easter Morning	220
We'll Never Say Good-Bye	20
Wonderful Bible	52
Work for Jesus Everywhere	34
Working and Waiting	46
Who Is this King of Glory?	54
Who Will Gather?	153
Yes, We Have A Word	89

INDEX TO FIRST LINES.

Alleluia, sing to Jesus	177
All hail the power of	47
Angels from the realms of	203
Angel voices sweetly sounding	86
Ask, for the Father is ready	110
As oft with worn and weary feet	142
Banner of the blessed tree	28
Bathed in unfading sunlight	63
Before Jehovah's awful throne	59
Beyond the smiling	79
Blessed is He	164
Blest be the tie	39
Brightly gleams our banner	70
Callest thou thus	130
Christian, dost thou see them	84
Christ is risen!	206
Come and join our cheerful song	210
Come unto me	150
Clad in the gospel armor	178

Index to First Lines.

	PAGE
Daily, daily sing the	143
Do kind things promptly	42
Down the valley	166
Each cooing dove	94
Fierce is the tempest	15
Floating down the misty	188
Fresh from the throne of glory	61
Gethsemane, the place of prayer	48
Gladly toiling for the Master	100
God doth not bid thee wait	67
Golden harps are sounding	76
Great Captain of Salvation	37
Hail the day that sees Him rise	211
Hail to the springtime	208
Hark! bright angels sweetly sing	207
Hark! hark! my soul	180
Hark! I hear my Saviour say	107
Hark! 'tis the Shepherd's voice	108
Have you not a word	88
Hear the bugle calling	19
Hear the promise of	151
He leadeth me	139
Helpless I come to Jesus' blood	112
Ho, every one	169
Holy Spirit, Truth divine	87
How green is the hillside	122
How sweetly flowed	145
I am trusting Thee	102
I have read of a wonderful	74
I heard the voice	131
I know when the river I cross	118
I'm always rejoicing for	138
In our blessed cause	144
In Thee, O Lord	186
In the shadow of Thy wings	156
In the sunlight bright	65
In the midst of temptation	57
In the morn of morns, when we	20
In the happy land	25
In the shining home	140
Is it nothing to me?	106
Is thy cruse almost exhausted?	17
I was a wand'ring sheep	117
I was glad	160
I will bear my cross	92
I will go to Jesus now	104
Jehovah, He my Shepherd	147
Jehovah is my light	133
Jesus, and may I work for Thee?	43
Jesus, blessed Saviour	174
Jesus, Saviour, pilot me	53
Jesus, the very thought of	55
Jordan's waters fair	154
Joy, joy, joy! the Easter	218
Lead, kindly light	113
Leave behind earth's empty	103

	PAGE
Let loud hosannas joyful rise	60
Let us sing our Father's love	21
Life is coming	129
Lift me higher, blessed Jesus	96
Lift up your hearts to things above	114
Like a river glorious	121
List to the notes that the angels	200
Looking unto Jesus	111
Lord, give me light	99
Lord of my life	40
Lord, speak to me	77
Lord, we come	176
Lord! we come before Thee now	123
Lord, when we bend	93
Lo! the harvest field	153
Make room for the blessed	157
Mid scenes of confusion	23
Midst the dew-gem'd fields	191
Mighty army of the young	8
Nobody knows but Jesus	109
No, no, it is not dying	127
Not a mountain streamlet	64
Nothing to pay	175
Not to angels hath been	116
Now let us sing the	198
Now the day is over	73
O believer, now rejoice	159
O Christmas, merry Christmas	194
O come to the living stream	83
O day of rest and gladness	136
O'er the trackless deep the sailor	22
O fisherman, toiling in shallows	4
Oh, what a promise God has given	124
O Jesus, Thou art standing	128
O my sweet home, Jerusalem	137
On a starry night	192
On thee, O Jesus	101
On the well at Sychar	148
Onward, Christian soldiers	82
Onward, pilgrim, don't delay	24
O paradise	62
Opened are fountains of	98
O ring the glad bells	189
O Saviour, precious	126
Our God, our help	168
Our Lord is risen	213
Our sins on Christ were laid	141
O wanderer, cease thy straying	32
O why wilt thou longer delay	36
Peace on earth	204
Put on, put on the whole armor	68
Praise the Lord	170
Praise the Lord, our Redeemer	11
Praise ye	181
Praise ye the Lord, angels	44
Resting on the faithfulness	146
Ring happy bells of	212
Ring out the happy Easter	216

INDEX TO FIRST LINES.

	PAGE		PAGE
Saviour, Surety, Lamb of God	29	Trust in the Lord with all	33
Scattering precious seed	72	Twine the Easter garland	209
See amid the winter's snow	190		
Show me, O Lord	78	Up! away! help tell the story	50
Singing for Jesus, our Saviour	56		
Sit down beneath the shadow	120	Waiting at the gates	10
Softly now the light of day	91	Wait, my soul, upon the Lord	85
Sun of my soul	75	Walk in the light, so shalt thou know	18
Springs of life in desert places	134	We are marching, we are	30
Stretch forth thy hand	97	We are soldiers of the cross	13
Sweet is the work, my God	149	Welcome Easter morning	220
Sweet the moments, rich in blessing	3	We march to victory	184
		We will sing the dear old	196
Take my life and let it be	105	When all Thy mercies	31
The blessed old banner	38	When I awake in the sweet morn	5
The Master is come	115	When like a stranger	155
There is a green hill far away	125	When this poor heart is burdened	135
There are bright shining lights	6	When we rise to greet	214
There is a land from sorrow free	14	While the sky of life	90
There is sunlight in my soul	119	Who is this King of glory?	54
There's a blessing for me	69	Who plants along a wayside	66
There's a land that is fairer	158	Wonderful Bible, book of all	52
There's a thrill in the air	202	Work for Jesus everywhere	34
There's a wonderful story	26	Working for the Master	46
This is not my place of resting	51	Why go around with troubled	152
This same Jesus! Oh, how sweetly	132		
Thou art coming	80	Ye sons and daughters of the	217
Thro' the yesterday of ages	12	Yes, we have a word	89
Trav'ler, wither art thou going	58	You who are called to the feast	16

INDEX OF SUBJECTS.

ANNIVERSARY.—8, 11, 13, 18, 19, 24, 30, 34, 40, 44, 56, 60, 64, 70, 72, 82, 100, 126, 154, 160, 164, 170, 178, 181, 184.
BENEVOLENCE.—17, 21, 31, 40, 43.
CHILDREN'S DAY.—8, 18, 30, 34, 44, 60, 64, 70, 72, 148, 154, 160, 164, 170, 184.
CHRISTMAS.—188, 189, 190, 192, 194, 196, 198, 200, 202, 203, 204.
EASTER.—206, 207, 208, 209, 210, 211, 212, 213, 214, 216, 217, 218, 220.
DEVOTIONAL.—3, 5, 12, 18, 21, 23, 24, 25, 28, 31, 33, 37, 38, 40, 42, 44, 47, 52, 54, 60, 61, 65, 66, 67, 68, 69, 74, 76, 77, 78, 79, 82, 85, 88, 89, 90, 92, 94, 99, 101, 126, 160.
HEAVEN.—6, 10, 14, 20, 22, 23, 25, 51, 57, 58, 61, 62, 63, 86, 90, 92, 96, 103, 114, 137, 140, 143, 156, 158.
INVITATION.—3, 4, 32, 36, 83, 85, 88, 97, 110, 112, 130, 131, 148, 150, 157.
MISSIONARY.—4, 15, 28, 37, 38, 43, 50, 72, 82, 100, 153, 178.
PRAISE.—11, 13, 21, 24, 25, 40, 44, 47, 54, 59, 60, 65, 66, 69, 70, 73, 74, 75, 76, 80, 82, 85, 92, 93, 94, 99, 100, 102, 113, 114, 115, 121, 123, 126, 129, 132, 136, 138, 144, 146, 160, 164, 168, 170, 174, 177, 180, 181, 184, 186.
REVIVAL.—3, 4, 5, 6, 8, 10, 12, 15, 16, 17, 18, 20, 22, 23, 24, 25, 26, 28, 29, 32, 36, 43, 46, 47, 48, 50, 51, 53, 57, 58, 61, 62, 63, 64, 65, 69, 72, 74, 78, 83, 84, 85, 86, 87, 88, 89, 90, 92, 96, 97, 98, 99, 100, 102, 104, 105, 106, 107, 108, 109, 110, 111, 112, 113, 114, 118, 128, 130, 131, 132, 135, 137, 138, 139, 140, 141, 144, 148, 150, 151, 152, 156, 157, 158, 159, 175.
THE SAVIOUR.—3, 5, 8, 12, 15, 16, 29, 33, 37, 43, 47, 48, 53, 54, 75, 78, 80, 83, 101, 102, 104, 105, 106, 107, 111, 112, 115, 122, 126, 128, 131, 132, 135, 138, 146, 152, 157, 159, 164, 174, 175.
THE SCRIPTURES.—52, 99, 151.
WORK.—4, 13, 19, 24, 28, 30, 34, 39, 43, 46, 50, 68, 70, 77, 82, 84, 100, 103, 108, 115, 116, 138, 144, 149, 151, 153, 176, 178.

www.ingramcontent.com/pod-product-compliance
Lightning Source LLC
Chambersburg PA
CBHW021843230426
43669CB00008B/1067